T0326250

Praise for *Elegant Failure*

"It's refreshing to read intelligent reflections on the Zen tradition that come from a true grounding in life and practice rather than mere intellectual interest."

—Zen Master Dae Kwang, Abbot, International Kwan Um
School of Zen, and senior editor of *Primary Point*,
Journal of the Kwan Um School of Zen

"Full of Zen stories both from historical times and from his own current experience, Richard Shrobe (Zen Master Wu Kwang) weaves a poetic tapestry of the old with the new. In *Elegant Failure* we have the opportunity to experience the relevance of kong-ans that could otherwise be perceived as esoteric. It is as though the ancient worthies are still alive today, living in New York City, speaking their timeless truth through the voice of one of the great living Zen masters in America today. Excellent!"

—Zen Master Jane Dobisz, Guiding Teacher,
Cambridge Zen Center, and author of *The Wisdom of Silence*

"A generous and insightful guide and commentary on Zen kong-ans. Because of his many years of practice, Richard has the ability to point directly to the marrow of these ancient teachings."

—Zen Master Soeng Hyang (Barbara Rhodes),
School Zen Master, International Kwan Um School of Zen

"Richard Shrobe's *Elegant Failure* extends the tradition of kong-an commentary into the current situation, exposing these old Zen enigmas one by one as the stories of our lives. His writing is informed, personal, and deeply rooted in practice. A brilliant success."
—Stanley Lombardo, Professor of Classics, University of Kansas, and editor of *Zen Sourcebook: Traditional Documents from China, Korea and Japan*

"With wisdom, deep learning and unshakable integrity, Zen Master Richard Shrobe presents the old masters in all their strangeness and familiarity. Fully human, fully alive, without explicit exhortation, he and they urge us to wake up right now to our original nature."
—Judy Roitman, Guiding Teacher, Kansas Zen Center, and editor of *Zen Sourcebook: Traditional Documents from China, Korea and Japan*

Elegant Failure

Elegant Failure

A Guide to Zen Koans

Richard Shrobe

SHAMBHALA • BOULDER • 2010

Shambhala Publications, Inc.
2129 13th Street
Boulder, Colorado 80302
www.shambhala.com

A Rodmell Press book

Printed in the United States of America

Shambhala Publications makes every effort to print on acid-free, recycled paper.

Shambhala Publications is distributed worldwide by Penguin Random House, Inc., and its subsidiaries.

Editors: Holly Hammond, Donald Moyer
Design and cover illustration: Gopa & Ted2, Inc.
Indexer: Ty Koontz
Production Editor: Linda Cogozzo
Author Photo: David Shrobe
Text set in Guardi LT Std 9.6/15

Library of Congress Cataloging-in-Publication Data
Wu, Kwang. Elegant failure: a guide to Zen koans/Richard Shrobe. 1st ed. Berkeley, Calif.: Rodmell Press.
xi, 244 p.; 23 cm.
BQ9289.5.W82 2010
ISBN 978-1-930485-25-9

Dedication

In memory of J.W. Harrington, executive administrative director, Kwan Um School of Zen, who embodied helpfulness, kindness, and unceasing diligent effort.

Contents

Acknowledgments

I want to express my appreciation for the efforts of my editors, John Holland and Elizabeth McGuinness, who were able to retain the lively (I hope) conversational style of the original dharma talks while making the material flow in readable form. My grateful thanks also go to Mary Ekwall, Sonya Lazarevic, Eugene Lim, Daniel Michael, and Jeff Timmins for their painstaking work in transcribing the original material, and to Clare Ellis, Eugene Lim, Nick Gershberg, and Paul Majchrzyk for reading the final manuscript and providing many useful ideas and suggestions.

I bow to my teacher, the late Seung Sahn Dae Soen Sa Nim, whose encouragement, compassion, and clarity continue to flow to me and to countless others.

Introduction

You shall no longer take things at second or third hand, nor look
through eyes of the dead, nor feed on the spectres in books,
You shall not look through my eyes either, nor take things from me,
You shall listen to all sides and filter them from your self.
I have heard what the talkers were talking, the talk of the
beginning and the end,
But I do not talk of the beginning or the end.

—Walt Whitman, *Song of Myself*

The term *kong-an* (*koan* in Japanese) is typically translated as "a case of public record." The concept was borrowed from the ancient Chinese legal system, where a case of public record set a precedent. Later legal issues of a similar kind could then be weighed and tested against the earlier precedent. Zen kong-ans usually recount sayings of ancient masters or interchanges between a master and student or between two masters. Occasionally a kong-an is based on a short section of Buddhist scripture or an allegorical tale of interaction between humans and a deity or supernatural being. Some of these interchanges and tales were recorded and used by subsequent generations of Zen teachers as teaching tools for their students. The cases that stood the test of time were eventually compiled into collections in China between the tenth and thirteenth centuries. So the Zen kong-an, like the legal kong-an, became a case of public record that later generations could use to test their clarity and insight by "looking into the old cases."

However, unlike legal cases, Zen cases are not meant to be studied intellectually, analyzed, or approached using the usual style of conceptual thinking. The Zen kong-an acts as an experiential learning tool. It is used as a prod to encourage the Zen student to wake up, stay awake, and engage with the actual universe of experience, rather than clinging to self-constructed concepts and opinions. By stripping away previously accumulated ideas and knowledge, the kong-an points the Zen student directly toward facets of spiritual perception, functioning, and relationships.

Kong-ans are probably best known for their unusual use of language and for the seemingly nonrational quality of their dialogues. For this reason, kong-ans are often described as riddles or paradoxes. Or they are viewed as encrypted capsules of spiritual wisdom that can be penetrated only by those of special ability or after many long years of difficult struggle. Zen Master Wu-men (Mumon; Mu Mun), the compiler of the *Wu-men-kuan*, spent six years as a young monk struggling with Chao-Chou's "Mu" kong-an, sometimes wandering the temple at night and knocking his head against the stone pillars in an attempt to break through. Most Zen students have experienced at some level this feeling of frustration and self-doubt that kong-an work engenders. However, once the point of the kong-an is perceived, we realize that we have been struggling not with the kong-an but with one of our many illusory opinions. As Wu-men points out in his preface to the *Wu-men-kuan*, "There is no gate from the beginning."

When I worked on kong-ans with my teacher, Zen Master Seung Sahn, he taught me by example the value of self-reliance, and he approached even the kong-ans of the ancient masters with a healthy degree of skepticism, which has always existed in the Zen tradition. For example, Zen practitioners may be tempted to regard every case in *The Blue Cliff Record* as having equal weight. It was therefore refreshing to have my teacher periodically remark, "This case not so interesting." Or he would indicate that some particular case was almost the same as a previous case we had worked through. Further, he would sometimes comment on the dialogues in the kong-ans, saying, "This dharma combat not so clear." Then he would pause and say, "But at the time it was clear." On other occasions his eyes would get bright, and he would exclaim, "Ah! This case *very* interesting!" After I had struggled through, he would point out the alternative ways of seeing what was being alluded to in the kong-an.

Based on my experience working with kong-ans for over thirty years, I have selected a group of cases for this book that I have found to be deeply meaningful and helpful to Zen practice. While there is no substitute for doing kong-an work in the interview room, kong-ans are also teaching tales. The material in them can be unpacked and presented in ways that can make them more accessible and meaningful to Zen students and other readers without losing the original spirit and without falling into intellectual analysis or speculation. Therefore, for each kong-an, I have presented both the traditional Zen teaching points and anecdotes that illuminate the kong-an's connection to modern everyday life—or to Zen as "ordinary mind." In the years that I have been giving talks on the kong-ans, listeners have often commented afterward that they had previously found kong-ans to be remote and impenetrable, and that they had not realized how these cases related to their everyday lives. It is my hope that these chapters will open your eyes to the different layers of meaning contained in these kong-ans, and that this will serve to aid and encourage your spiritual practice.

Kong-an Collections: A Brief Background

Traditionally there are said to be 1,700 kong-ans. From these, three main kong-an collections emerged in China during the Sung Dynasty (960–1280 CE). These are *The Blue Cliff Record,* containing 100 cases, the *Wu-men-kuan* (*Mumonkan; Mu Mun Kwan*), containing 48 cases, and the *Book of Serenity,* which also contains 100 cases and is used primarily by the Soto Zen sect. These three collections share a number of cases in common. Most of the kong-ans in this book are taken from *The Blue Cliff Record,* along with a few from the *Wu-men-kuan.*

The Blue Cliff Record was originally compiled by Zen Master Hsueh-tou (Setcho) in the first half of the eleventh century. Hsueh-tou selected 100 kong-ans, to which he added short verses and occasional brief comments. About a hundred years later, Zen Master Yuan-wu (Engo) elaborated on Hsueh-tou's work by adding an introduction to each case, frequent short comments, a dharma discourse on the main case, and a dharma discourse on Hsueh-tou's verse. Yuan-wu's version of *The Blue Cliff Record* is a multilayered work with many subtleties of meaning, so much so that, shortly after its completion, it began to be used as the province of intellectual study and speculation. It was for this reason that Yuan-wu's successor, Zen Master Ta-hui (Daie), gathered all the copies that he could find and had them burned. Ta-hui's motivation was "better to preserve the core intent of his master's teaching, which was certainly not about intellectual speculation, than to preserve his master's volume."

The *Wu-men-kuan*, compiled during the thirteenth century (ca. 1229 CE), is a much simpler work. Zen Master Wu-men gathered forty-eight kong-ans, to which he added a short commentary and a verse. Many teachers favor Wu-men's collection, due to its directness and clarity. Often the dialogues in *The Blue Cliff Record* seem opaque, in need of a good deal of clarification; not so with most of the cases in the *Wu-men-kuan*.

Structure of the Book

The teachings in these chapters were originally presented in dharma talks to the Zen students of the Chogye International Zen Center of New York. The edited transcriptions of these talks form the chapters of this book. The cases are organized into three sections. Chapters 1 through 5 contain kong-ans involving Zen masters from the early period of Zen in China. These teachers were active shortly after the time of the Sixth Patriarch and are regarded as the precursors of the five main schools, or houses, of Zen. Chapters 6 through 18 contain kong-ans connected with teachers from these five main schools or, in a few cases, an immediate predecessor. Chapters 19 through 22 contain kong-ans that are based on short sections from the Buddhist scriptures or from a fable or mystery tale.

I begin each chapter with a four-line encapsulated presentation of the essence of the kong-an, following the Korean Zen style for beginning a formal Dharma speech. In practice, the Zen Master holds the Zen stick in the air, hits the lectern, and then presents the first line. This is repeated before the second and third lines, followed by the traditional Zen shout (Katz! or Ho! or Haahh!), a deep, penetrating sound coming from the gut that is intended to wipe away all traces of conceptual thought. The last line is then presented, a sentence that reveals the true meaning "just as it is."

The translations of *The Blue Cliff Record* and the *Wu-men-kuan* that I have used as the starting point for this book are by my teacher, Zen Master Seung Sahn. Zen Master Seung Sahn's translation of *The Blue Cliff Record* is limited to the main cases, and his translation of the *Wu-men-kuan* includes the cases and verses but omits Wu-men's commentary. When referring to comments, discourses, or verses not translated by Zen Master Seung Sahn, I have used other sources, as noted. Zen Master Seung Sahn is not the only teacher to view the main case as what is most vitally important. In *Crooked Cucumber*, a biography of Shunryu Suzuki Roshi, I remember reading a short dharma talk by the Zen master on a kong-an from *The Blue Cliff Record* in which he also focused on the main case alone, with no reference to the introduction, verse, or incidental comments.

For the names of the masters in these kong-ans, I have used the Chinese form, but I have also included the Japanese and Korean equivalents wherever possible. This is because in the West we now have strong practicing communities from all three traditions who are familiar with the teachings of our Zen ancestors.

CHAPTER I

Yen-kuan's Rhinoceros Fan

*If you attain the fundamental point, then you understand
that the horn on the top of its head is sharp.*

*If you don't stop there, but move past, then it becomes clear:
Wind blows, pinetree shakes.*

However, these two are not yet complete.

What is it that completes these two?

Haahh!!

In winter it chills to the bone. In springtime it caresses the skin.

Case 91 of *The Blue Cliff Record* states:

One day Yen Kuan called to his attendant, "Bring me my
rhinoceros fan."

The attendant said, "The fan is broken."

Yen Kuan said, "If the fan is broken, bring the rhinoceros
back to me."

The attendant had no reply.[1]

Hsueh-tou (Setcho), the compiler of *The Blue Cliff Record*, then added
responses from other monks to Yen-kuan's (Enkan; Yom Kwan)

challenge to produce the rhinoceros and also added his own short comments to each response:

> T'ou-tzu said, "I do not refuse to bring it out, but I fear the horn on its head will be imperfect."
> Hsueh-tou commented, "I want an imperfect horn."
> Shih-shuang said, "If I return the rhino to the Master, then I won't have it."
> Hsueh-tou commented, "The rhino is still there."
> Tzu-fu drew a circle and wrote the word *rhino* inside it.
> Hsueh-tou commented, "Why did you not bring it out?"
> Pao-fu said, "The Master is aged; someone else is good."
> Hsueh-tou commented, "What a pity—such hard work with no merit."[2]

At first glance, this case may seem bewildering. I once presented it to one of my students in the interview room. He said, "I read that case several years ago, and I said to myself, I hope I'm never asked about this!" As the presentation is somewhat complex, I will explain what is going on here.

Zen Master Yen-kuan was a dharma successor of Zen Master Ma-tsu (Baso; Ma Jo), but few details of his life have come down to us beyond the fact that he owned a fan. According to different commentators, the handle of the fan was made from a rhinoceros horn, or the ribs on the fan were made from rhinoceros horn, or the fan itself had a picture of a rhinoceros with its horn sticking up, pointing at a full moon.

The verbal fencing over the fan between Yen-kuan and his attendant is what we usually refer to as dharma combat. The first response, "The fan is broken," is considered a pretty good one; I will explain why a little later. But when Yen-kuan challenged his attendant a second time, saying, "Well, if the fan is broken, then bring the rhino here," the attendant had nothing more to say. When that happens, zennists say your head is a dragon, but your tail is a snake: You came on strongly at first, but when challenged you could not maintain that energy. From being a roaring dragon, you became a common, ordinary garden snake.

Sometimes a kong-an is straightforward, involving no symbolism. But in other instances, objects are used to represent something else. Here several words have symbolic meanings: *rhino*, *fan*, and *broken*.

The Chinese used to consider the rhinoceros a kind of ox. In the Zen tradition, the ox is often used as a representation of mind. A series of ox-herding pictures from Sung Dynasty China depict ten stages, or aspects, of the path to complete realization, using the image of an ox and rider.

Then, the fan: Remember that a fan makes wind. In the Zen tradition, the image of wind is often used to represent something that is all-pervading, that covers everything. But if you do not have a fan to make it, you never experience the nature of the wind here and now. Conversely wind sometimes represents complications, as in stirring up things or making waves.

Finally, the word *broken*: In the Korean tradition particularly but also in the Chinese tradition, *broken* may refer to an enlightening experience. Here is where we realize why the answer "The fan is broken" was a good one. In this context, *broken* has several different nuances or synonyms connected with it. One is to wake up. Another is to become sober. A line in the Buddhist precept ceremony says, "Generation after generation, we exist in a stupor, as one drunk." So to become sober means to come out of that stupor and to see clearly.

Another synonym of *broken* is "to be aware." Once a student asked a Zen master, "What is the essence of the Zen way?" The Zen master said, "Attention!" The student said, "And after that?" The master said, "Attention!" The student said, "And after that?" The master said, "Attention." The student, one more time, said, "And then what?" The master said, "Attention."

Often people think that attention means developing some intense power of concentration, as you might see among certain Indian yogis who can sit totally still and stay inwardly absorbed. You could drop a bomb next to them, and they might not even hear it. Or like a Chinese kung-fu master, who has such intense concentration that he would be immovable if you tried to push him over. Some people think that is the kind of attention required in the Zen tradition. But that is not really the idea.

For us, attention primarily has to do with caring. If you attend to something, you care for it and give time to it. To give time and attention is to give caring. To pay attention to the mundane, simple, small details of everyday life is to live in the world with a spirit of caring, as if each and every thing were in your stewardship, as if you have a responsibility to care for every moment and each thing. That attitude expresses an absolute valuing of all experience. Attention, from the Zen point of view, has much more to do with caring than with some strong, focused concentration. It is true that when we sit in meditation we pay attention, with a certain kind of focusing and stabilizing of energy. But primarily attention is about caring and being careful. And ultimately, caring means to become one with the object of care. So, connected with this word *broken* is the aspect of attending to and becoming sober.

Broken also may suggest hatched, like a chicken hatching. A monk said to Zen Master Ching-ch'ing (Kyosei; Gyeong Cheong), "Master, I'm pecking out. You, please, peck in." That offers an image of student and teacher in accord with each other: I'm trying to break out. You, please, break in, so the two of us together can connect, mind to mind. Ching-ch'ing shouted at the monk, "Are you alive or not?" That was his pecking in.

Broken essentially points toward breaking through the tight net of our conditioning and our colored views and just seeing clearly what is here. So when Yen-kuan says, "If the fan is broken, bring the rhinoceros back to me," that means, if you've really broken through, then show me. But the monk can't say anything. The wind is not yet blowing freely there.

Then these other fellows offer their comments. T'ou-tzu (Tosu; Tu Ja) says, "I do not refuse to bring it out [meaning the rhinoceros], but I fear the horn on its head will be imperfect." That seems to be about hesitancy and holding back: I would bring it out, but I'm afraid that the horn on its head might not be up to par; it might be an imperfect horn. That is the kind of answer we get when checking-mind appears, making-good-and-bad appears, making-better-and-worse appears, and when holding back emerges. For example, someone said to me recently, "I've been trying to get around to balancing my checkbook for the last six months." I said, "How come you didn't get to it sooner?" The answer was, "I'm always afraid it won't come out right!"

Then Hsueh-tou, replying to T'ou-tzu, says, "I want an imperfect horn."

Maybe a story or two will help explain Hsueh-tou's reply. Once when I was at the Providence Zen Center to commemorate Buddha's enlightenment, a participant from Lithuania said, "In Lithuania, we never had any Zen or Buddhism until about 1991 or 1992, when one of the teachers from the Kwan Um Zen School visited. Then a few of us began practicing, but there were no resident teachers: We had to rely on what we learned the few times a teacher from the United States came through. So from the very beginning, we had to try to show new people how to practice, even though we had very little experience and our own understanding was raw and imperfect. We had to immediately start teaching meditation and something about the spirit of Zen practice and the Zen way of living. From the very beginning, we had to be both teachers and students."

One of Zen Master Seung Sahn's first American students also has a similar tale to tell. In the early 1970s, when Seung Sahn first came to the United States, he was living in Providence, Rhode Island, and had a connection with a professor from Brown University. Occasionally Seung Sahn would be invited to give a talk before a gathering of university professors. This student would often go along, hoping to hear the talk. "We were all very new to this," he says. "Zen Master Seung Sahn himself had only been here for maybe six months or a year." They would travel to the university and sit down with the group. But sometimes, instead of beginning a talk, Seung Sahn would turn and say, "You give a dharma talk." At first the student would cringe and want to hide and would not know what to say; then he would somehow squeeze out something of what he had been practicing and learning.

That is in the spirit of "I want to see the imperfect horn." It is giving freely, not holding back, not hesitating. Or, in spite of the hesitation and wanting to hide, just doing it anyway, without being hindered by thoughts of good and bad.

Then Shih-shuang (Sekiso; Sok Sahn), the second monk whose comments are included in the kong-an, says, "If I return the rhino to the master, then I won't have it." The first response—"I fear the horn will be imperfect"—is about the fear of looking stupid. The second is about losing something: If I give it to you, then I won't have it.

Some years ago, I worked in a drug rehab program that had a slogan: Give it away in order to keep it. As new addicts would come into the program, people who had been clean and sober longer would help the new people—give it away. There is always this fear of losing something. But essentially, if you are going to practice the Zen way, you have to lose all your hopes and all your expectations.

When I started practicing in my midtwenties, my teacher was Swami Satchidananda, a guru of the Yoga Vedanta tradition. In early adulthood, my guru had been a family person, with a wife and children. Around age twenty-eight, he developed a powerful commitment to the goal of attaining self-realization and left his family, to become a swami, or monk. In Asian countries, of course—in countries where they have had monastic traditions for centuries—that is accepted by society. If you leave home with an attitude of sincerity, the extended family takes up the care of those left behind and raises your children. At least that is the way it is reported to be.

When I began practicing, my wife was also practicing, but I began to have the idea that she was not as zealous a student as I was. I began to think, My wife may become a hindrance to my practice; she may not really support it adequately. So I made this secret promise to myself: When I get to the age of twenty-eight, if she hasn't come up to my standards, I will leave her and become a monk. I don't think I've ever shared this with her. Anyway, twenty-eight came and went, and now I have been married for over forty years. I recognized that my practice was learning to live with the fact that she was not going to practice the way I was practicing, and learning to give up my expectation about the way I wanted her to practice.

A student told me about going to a growth workshop of some kind, at which participants were expected to make commitments to themselves about intentions they were going to pursue. This person's intention was, By the time I get to age such-and-such, I will have completed the course of kong-an study and practice. That is all about expectation.

If you walk the path of Zen, many hopes and expectations will fall away. Sometimes they won't fall away easily; you will go through a crisis of faith. It is necessary, over and over again, to reconnect at those times with the spirit of why you started practicing in the first place, the attitude of beginner's mind. That is called intention, or vow. And that is the essence of the spirit of practice.

At the end of the case is a poem by Hsueh-tou:

> You have long used the rhinoceros fan.
> ["Long used" means forever, before the beginning.]
>   If asked, however, you know nothing of it.
> [You know nothing of it because it is not something out there; it is your very being, your self.]
>   Infinite, the cool breeze, and the head and horns,
>   Like clouds and rain which have passed, it cannot be captured.[3]

This means you cannot make an object out of your essential being. You cannot grasp hold of your self. The Diamond Sutra says, "Past mind is ungraspable, present mind is ungraspable, future mind is ungraspable."

I hope that we all realize the imperfect horn on our heads, lose every hindrance and encumbrance, and actualize clarity and compassion.

Notes

1. Seung Sahn, trans., *The Blue Cliff Record* (Cumberland, RI: Kwan Um School of Zen, 1983), 69.
2. Ibid.
3. Katsuki Sekida, trans., *Two Zen Classics: Mumonkan and Hekiganroku* (New York: Weatherhill, 1977), 380.

CHAPTER 2

Ma-ku's Two-Place Ring Staff

At the zero point is there correct and incorrect?
At this point is there right and is there wrong?
Can you use this point freely or does it stand as a hindrance?
Where in all this will you find the true gate?
Haahh!!
The front door leads to the garden. The flowers are red and yellow.

You may see some aspects of yourself depicted in this story, case 31 in *The Blue Cliff Record*, about Ma-ku (Mayoku; Ma Gok) and the two Zen masters whom he visited, or in the commentator, Hsüeh-tou (Setcho). It's like looking at a brief allegory or psychodrama of your mind.

Ma Ku, carrying his ring-staff, went to Chang Ching. He circled the meditation seat three times, struck his staff once, and stood there upright. Chang Ching said, "Correct. Correct."
(Hsüeh-tou [the commentator] added a word, saying, "Wrong!")
Ma Ku also went to Nan Ch'uan. He circled the meditation seat three times, struck his staff once, and stood there upright. Nan Ch'uan said, "Not correct. Not correct."

(Hsüeh-tou added a word, saying, "Wrong!")

Ma Ku then said, "Chang Ching said 'Correct.' Why do you say, 'Not correct,' Master?"

Nan Ch'uan said, "Chang Ching is correct; it's you who are not correct. This is what the wind-power turns around. Finally, it breaks down and disappears."[1]

We have four people here: Ma-ku, Chang-ch'ing (Shokyo; Jang Gyeong), Nan-ch'uan (Nansen; Nam Cheon), and Hsueh-tou (Set-cho), who is the collector of these stories and the compiler of *The Blue Cliff Record.* He organized this collection several hundred years after these events happened, adding occasional comments and short poems. Later masters interjected their comments, offering their stamps of approval as it were, or putting in their two cents' worth. At the time this incident occurred, traveling monks would carry long walking staffs, on top of which were usually twelve rings that jingled, especially when the staff hit the ground. The twelve rings were said to represent the twelve links in the chain of causation, according to traditional Buddhism, and also the twelve meditation gates that are mentioned in a particular sutra. Ma-ku, Chang-ch'ing, and Nan-ch'uan were all students of the great teacher Ma-tsu (Baso; Ma Jo) (709–788).

The potential snares of the story are: "Correct. Correct." "Not correct. Not correct." Followed by "Wrong! Wrong!" Fundamentally there is just one clear point: Ma-ku hitting the ground with his staff.

Ma-ku's circling the meditation seat, hitting his staff, and standing upright was not the usual style of greeting a Zen master; it was a breech of formality. But Master Chang-ch'ing responds by saying, "Correct. Correct." Hsueh-tou's comment, however, is "Wrong." The story continues when Ma-ku calls on Nan-ch'uan, in front of whom he puts on the same play, and Nan-ch'uan says, "Not correct. Not correct." To this, Hsueh-tou adds the identical comment, "Wrong." The real question is, Who caught whom? If you relate to the sound of the ring staff hitting the ground as either correct or incorrect, you are already ten thousand miles from the point.

This story is similar to an incident involving the Sixth Patriarch that occurred a couple of hundred years earlier. A monk named Yung-chia (Yoka) came to call on the Sixth Patriarch, Hui-neng (E'no). He walked around the Sixth Patriarch three times, hit his stick, and stood there upright. As this was not the customary way for a monk to meet the master of a temple, the Sixth Patriarch said to him, "Where is it that you come from, filled with such conceit? A monk is supposed to observe the rules of propriety." Yung-chia said, "This matter of life and death is very serious. I don't have time for proprieties."

The dialogue between them continued a little longer, and the Sixth Patriarch eventually acknowledged that Yung-chia had some experience of realization. Then Yung-chia said, "Well, goodbye. I'm leaving," to which the Sixth Patriarch rejoined, "Don't you think you're leaving a little soon?" Yung-chia answered with another question, "Where is fast or slow in this matter?" After they had talked further, the Sixth Patriarch acknowledged more strongly that Yung-chia had full grasp of the essential point. Then he said, "Why don't you stay one night?" Yung-chia consented. Later he was referred to as the Overnight Enlightened Guest.

In our case, Ma-ku carries Chang-ch'ing's "correct, correct" with him as he goes to call on Nan-ch'uan. Then he performs the same drama, and Nan-ch'uan says, "Not correct. Not correct." Ma-ku questions, "Why do you say, 'Not correct'? Chang-ch'ing said, 'Correct.'" Nan-ch'uan retorts, "Chang-ch'ing is correct; it's you who are not correct. This is what the wind-power turns around. Finally it breaks down and disappears." We might say, You are full of hot air. And in the end, if you are inflated from somebody else's validation, it will easily disintegrate, because your confidence is not supported from within. You have not thoroughly digested your own experience. This is an important point. When Zen Master Seung Sahn gave one of his students sanction to teach (*inka*), he urged the fledgling teacher to visit Zen masters of other traditions and have interviews with them as part of the new teacher's training. I remember when I did it; I felt as if I were going into foreign territory and dealing with an unfamiliar vocabulary, because all Zen masters do not teach in the same format or style, even though perhaps the essence of what they are teaching is aimed at the same point. This custom of calling on other teachers after your teacher has given you approval originates in China at the time of this kong-an.

Once I went to sit a couple days of a *sesshin* with Sasaki Roshi, a Japanese Rinzai (Lin-chi) teacher. He was conducting a seven-day sesshin, but I entered toward the end of the retreat. I had been told that, in this Japanese style, when you went for a private interview with the Zen master you bowed to him and told him what kong-an you were working on. If you did not have a kong-an, you told him that, and he would give you one.

That evening I joined the sitting meditation and waited my turn for an interview with the master. When it came, I went into his room, bowed, and said, "Roshi, I've just arrived and have no kong-an." He straightened himself up, looked at me, and said, "Oh! Just now coming from where?" I immediately shouted, "Haahh!!" (This shout was used by Rinzai Zen masters to point to or reveal the mind before thinking arises.) The roshi quickly rang the bell, meaning, "The interview is over. Get out." Formality requires that you bow before leaving the room, so I bowed to him. While I was doing it, he took his Zen stick, hit me lightly on the back a couple of times, and said, "Don't act crazy." Bear in mind, I had already been teaching for three or four years in the Kwan Um School of Zen, in which "Where are you coming from?" is a preliminary kong-on—although one could obviously use it throughout life.

The next morning, we began sitting again. I wondered, Now, did Roshi want me to really work on that as a kong-an, "Where are you coming from?" Or was he just seizing the moment to make some dharma combat with me? Gee, I really don't know. When I went for another interview, I said, "Roshi, I just arrived last night, but I have no kong-an." He said, "I gave you a kong-an, but you are too stupid to realize it!" I said, "Yes, last night you said, 'Where are you coming from?'" He said, "Yes, I am a Rinzai teacher; your teacher is also from the same line. So where are you coming from?"

Sometimes you get praised, sometimes you get told what a stupid ass you are. But the question is, how much can you just keep your own center and flow with whatever is happening. That is what this kong-an is pointing at. Ma-ku, however, became attached to Chang-ch'ing's approval. Later Nan-ch'uan said, "Not correct," and Ma-ku began to dispute. "Chang-ch'ing said 'Correct.' Why do you say, 'Not correct'?" Nan-ch'uan then retorted, "Chang-ch'ing is correct. It's you who are not correct!"

In that, I think, we can all see something of ourselves—becoming defensive and prideful.

A later master wrote a comment after the first line in the case—the one telling how Ma-ku came calling on Chang-ch'ing, circled the meditation seat three times, hit his staff, and stood there motionless. This commentator wrote, "He sure has a lot of Chan [Zen.]"[2] That's a problem, to be too attached to Zen.

A couple of poems are attached to this case. The poem in *The Blue Cliff Record*, written by Zen Master Hsueh-tou, says:

> This "wrong" and that "wrong,"
> It is important not to take them away.
> Then the waves are calm in the four seas,
> The hundred rivers return to the ocean tide.
> The standard of the ancient rod is lofty, with twelve
>   gates;
> In each gate there is a road, empty and desolate.
> Not desolate—
> The adept should seek medicine without disease.[3]

An alternate translation of the same poem clarifies certain points:

> This mistake, that mistake,
> Never take them away!
> In the four seas, the waves subside;
> A hundred rivers flow quietly to the sea.
>
> The twelve bells of the staff tinkled up high;
> Empty and silent is the road to the gate.

No, not empty and silent;
The enlightened man must take medicine
For the illness of "having no illness."[4]

A few lines in the two versions deserve special attention. The original mind point is essentially empty and silent. There is nothing there. You cannot say correct, you cannot say incorrect; you cannot say right, you cannot say wrong; you cannot say inside, you cannot say outside. There is just one great, flowing silence. But if you cling to that silence, then you cannot help anyone, not even yourself. So Hsueh-tou says, "Empty and silent is the road to the gate."

Then he takes it back: "No, not empty and silent. / The enlightened man must take medicine / For the illness of 'having no illness.'" This zero point means no illness, nothing. But if you think you have no illness, that is an illness. If you can feel the sickness of this world and respond compassionately and skillfully to it, that is going beyond silent and empty. That is the source of compassionate action, and it is the direction of Zen practice.

One more poem connected with this case comes from *Book of Serenity*. It says:

Right and wrong—
Watch out for the trap.
Seeming to put down, seeming to uphold,
It's hard to tell who is the elder brother, who the younger.
Conceding, he adapts to the time;
Denying, what's special to me?
One shake of the metal staff—standing out all alone;
Three times around the seat, a leisurely romp.
The monasteries agitated 'right' and 'wrong' are born;
It seems like they're seeing ghosts in front of their skulls.[5]

Hsueh-tou wrote in the previous poem about these two wrongs that it is important not to take them away. This kong-on has a pair of absolutes: the absolute of "One shake of the metal staff—standing out all alone," and the absolute of "Wrong! Wrong!"

One of my students told a fable that may help illustrate what this absolute wrong is referring to. There were two frogs in a huge steel bowl. The bowl was filled halfway with milk. The frogs tried to get up the sides of the metal bowl but could not; the sides were slippery and too steep. The frogs realized that they would eventually drown in the milk. One frog was intelligent and the other was stupid. The intelligent frog saw immediately, "There's no way to get out of this, so there's no point in making any effort at all. I'll just give up right now and drown. That's the intelligent thing to do." And that is what it did. *Puk!* Dead!

The second frog, being stupid, decided, "I have to paddle, I have to try, no matter what." So it paddled and paddled and paddled and paddled with its frog legs. The webs on its legs acted as a churn, and the milk gradually, gradually congealed. Eventually it became butter, and the frog got a foothold and jumped out.

Relying only on intelligence limits the possibilities. If instead you just act completely, with no idea about whether the outcome will be correct or incorrect, then you enter the realm of absolute wrong, and then surprise is possible. If there is no surprise in life, then there is a problem. Surprise can be transformative.

In *Dropping Ashes on the Buddha,* Zen Master Seung Sahn tells another story about going the wrong way and surprise.[6] A stupid monk who lived in Korea about three hundred years ago was named Sok Du, which literally means "rock head." At first Sok Du tried studying the sutras, the scriptures. But they were way, way beyond him. He then decided he would try to be a Zen monk. Sitting Zen, however, was also way beyond him. So he settled on just working in the kitchen and on the temple grounds. Still, twice a month Sok Du would attend the dharma talks given by the Zen master, although each time he would be completely confused.

One day he went to the Zen master and said, "Master, I'm tired of being so stupid. Isn't there some way that I can understand?" The

Zen master said, "You must ask me a question." Sok Du thought and thought and thought. Finally he said, "You are always talking about Buddha. What is Buddha?" The Zen master answered, "Mind is Buddha." When spoken, the Chinese words for "Mind is Buddha" sound similar to "Buddha is grass shoes," straw sandals, and Sok Du misheard. "What a difficult kong-on," Sok Du thought. "How can Buddha be grass shoes? How will I ever understand 'Buddha is grass shoes'? What does it mean?" Every day after that, whatever he was doing—working in the kitchen or gathering firewood or working on the temple grounds—he continuously kept this big question: Buddha is grass shoes; what does that mean? He never went back to the Zen master to ask for clarification; he just kept the question. This went on for about three years.

Then one day, as he was walking down the hill to the temple, carrying a big bundle of firewood he had gathered on the mountainside, his foot hit a rock. As he tripped and tumbled, the firewood fell to the ground, and his straw sandals flew up in the air. When they hit the ground, the grass shoes completely broke apart. And at that, Sok Du had an awakening. He went running to the Zen master and said, "Master! Master, now I understand what Buddha is!" The Zen master looked at him and said, "Oh? Then what is Buddha?" Sok Du took one of the broken grass shoes and hit the master on the head. The Zen master said, "Is this the truth?" Sok Du said, "My shoes are all broken." The master burst out laughing, and Sok Du flushed with joy.

So not only are the grass shoes completely broken, but correct, correct is completely broken, not correct, not correct is completely broken, the staff hitting the ground is completely broken. Wrong, wrong is also completely broken.

I hope each of us pursues "wrong, wrong, never take that away," finds completely broken, and helps many beings.

Notes

1. Seung Sahn, trans., *The Blue Cliff Record* (Cumberland, RI: Kwan Um School of Zen, 1983), 26.

2. Thomas Cleary, trans., *Book of Serenity* (Boston: Shambhala, 1988), 70.

3. Thomas Cleary and J. C. Cleary, trans., *The Blue Cliff Record* (Boston: Shambhala, 1992), 199.

4. Katsuki Sekida, trans., *Two Zen Classics: Mumonkan and Hekiganroku* (New York: Weatherhill, 1977), 228.

5. Cleary, 68–69.

6. Seung Sahn, *Dropping Ashes on the Buddha* (New York: Grove, 1976), 83.

CHAPTER 3

Yao-shan's Elk of Elks

. . . .

*In ancient times, a wise man said, "I have one bow and
two arrows, and in twenty years I have been able to shoot
half a person." He then broke the bow and the two arrows.*

*When he said, "I have been able to shoot half a person," was he
referring to the side that was light or the side that was dark?
The side that was obvious or the side that was hidden?*

*If you understand the point of all this, then you too know
how to shoot and hit the target.*

But do you know how to hit yourself?

Haahh!!

Look carefully. Listen carefully.

. . . .

Zen Master Yao-shan (Yakusan; Yak Sahn), who was born in China
about 750 and died in 834, plays a leading role in the kong-an Elk of
Elks, case 81 of *The Blue Cliff Record:*

A monk asked Yao Shan, "On a level field, in the shallow grass,
the elk and deer form a herd; how can one shoot the elk of
elks?"

Yao Shan said, "Look—an arrow!"

The monk let himself fall down.

Yao Shan said, "Attendant, drag this dead wretch out."

The monk then ran out. Yao Shan said, "This wretch playing with a mud ball—when will it ever end?"

Hsueh-tou (Setcho), commented, saying, "Though living for three steps, must die in five steps."[1]

Yao-shan left home to become a monk when he was about sixteen and was fully ordained at twenty-four. He first studied the scriptural teachings and the philosophical treatises, becoming famed for his knowledge. Along with that, he scrupulously followed all the precepts of the monks' rules. When taking their final ordination, monks are given many major and minor precepts. Those who are really ortho-dox try to follow all the precepts meticulously. On the positive side, that is a way of practicing mindfulness in all activities, because there is a precept for everything—from which foot hits the floor first in the morning to what you do when you go to the toilet. In following these precepts meticulously, you have to pay attention. But there is a downside: You can become nit-picky, bound up in a bunch of rules, and not feel much of a sense of openness or spaciousness. Yao-shan practiced this way for several years but finally had a recognition that truth could not be found by precisely following the rules. That was when he decided to find a Zen master.

At that time, there were two great Zen masters teaching in China, Shih-t'ou (Sekito; Shi Hu) and Ma-tsu (Baso; Ma Jo). Each had stud-ied with one of the Sixth Patriarch's successors. All the various lin-eages that eventually became famous in Chinese Zen evolved from Shih-t'ou and Ma-tsu. So when Yao-shan set out, there were not many different styles proliferating. Yao-shan went to Shih-t'ou and said, "I understand the canonical teaching of Buddhism, but I hear that in Zen you teach looking into the essence of mind, realizing true nature, and becoming buddha. This I don't understand. Can you please explain it to me?" Shih-t'ou replied, "This way won't do; not this way won't do. Both this way and not this way won't do either. How about you?" Yao-shan was speechless and felt completely stuck.

In his response, Shih-t'ou had turned to the philosophical teachings of Buddhism—specifically, a classification called the four propositions. They identify four different aspects of everything we encounter: existence, nonexistence, both existence and nonexistence, and neither existence nor nonexistence. When you look at any phenomenon you encounter, you can say it exists—the first aspect. But look more deeply: Everything is changing, changing, changing, and passing away; you could say it does not really exist, it is like a dream. But asserting either one of these becomes a one-sided view, so there is a third postulate: It both exists and does not exist. All three of these, however, are still in the realm of conceptual thinking, so the ancient teachers posited a fourth: neither existing nor not existing. If it is neither existing nor not existing, then what?

When Shih-t'ou said to Yao-shan, "This way won't do; not this way won't do," he meant that looking at self as existing or not existing will not reveal true original self. Then, "How about you?" In that moment, he pointed Yao-shan right toward himself. If you cannot categorize yourself according to all the canonical teachings that you have learned, then what about you? What are you?

At that point Yao-shan's thinking was cut off, and he felt completely stuck. Shih-t'ou immediately said, "Your affinity is not here with me—go call on Ma-tsu for a while."

So Yao-shan set off. Don't think this was a short journey; it was probably hundreds of miles across the mountains of China. When Yao-shan arrived at Ma-tsu's temple, he asked Ma-tsu the same question: "I understand the canonical teaching of Buddhism, but I hear that in Zen you teach looking into the essence of mind, realizing true nature, and becoming buddha. This I don't understand. Can you please explain it to me?" Ma-tsu immediately said, "Sometimes I make him raise his eyebrows and blink his eyes. Sometimes I don't make him raise his eyebrows and blink his eyes. Sometimes raising his eyebrows and blinking his eyes is correct. And sometimes raising his eyebrows and blinking his eyes is not correct. How about you?" At that moment—*ptchh*—Yao-shan had an awakening experience.

What is the difference between Ma-tsu's teaching and Shih-t'ou's?

Ma-tsu is saying sometimes (meaning at a particular time, at a particular place, according to a particular circumstance), I make him raise his eyebrows and blink his eyes. Some other times, I don't have him do that (*him* referring to one's own being). Sometimes in a particular situation, to blink your eyes is correct action; sometimes it is not correct action. How about you? That means just now can you realize yourself in the activities of just seeing, just hearing, just lifting your eyebrows, just doing something in accord with the time and situation that you find yourself in?

Suddenly Yao-shan realized something, so he bowed to Ma-tsu. When Ma-tsu asked, "What have you realized that you bow to me?" Yao-shan said, "When I was at Shih-t'ou's place, it was like a mosquito trying to get a bite out of an iron ox," meaning that he could not find any entrance, "but what you've revealed to me in my activity here and now, I understand." Ma-tsu confirmed his perception at that moment and advised him of two things: "You've realized the truth, but guard it well. And even though you've realized the truth here with me, nevertheless your teacher is Shih-t'ou."

In Korea they say that when the rice is cooked, you should not immediately take the lid off; if you keep the lid on after you turn off the flame, the steam in the pot infiltrates and permeates the rice, so the rice takes on a particular consistency, texture, and fragrance. Only then is it fully done. If you take the lid off too soon, you lose something essential. Likewise, even though Yao-shan had some experience along the way, Ma-tsu tells him to guard it well. That applies to all of us in our practice. Don't take the lid off too soon.

After that, Yao-shan stayed with Ma-tsu for three years, serving as his attendant. One day Ma-tsu said to him, "You should leave here now and go to a high mountaintop and begin to teach." Yao-shan resisted the suggestion, saying, "Who am I to go and set up my own teaching?" Ma-tsu persisted and said, "If you don't begin to teach, your practice will not be complete." So Yao-shan first went back to Shih-t'ou, because his teacher had to confirm him as a teacher.

A story about Yao-shan and Shih-t'ou during that period tells how on one occasion when Yao-shan was sitting in meditation, Shih-t'ou came by and asked, "What are you doing?" Yao-shan replied, "I'm not doing anything." Shih-t'ou then said, "If you're not doing anything, then you are just sitting idly." Yao-shan retorted, "If I were sitting idly, I would be doing something." Shih-t'ou said, "You talk about not doing; what is it that you're not doing?" Yao-shan replied, "Even the ten thousand sages don't know."

In many stories, long before the kong-an technique was systematized and codified, Zen masters would point toward the mind of don't-know and don't-understand. It could be said that the original kong-an is "Don't know, don't understand." In a story about Zen Master Chao-chou (Joshu; Joju), one generation after Yao-shan, a student asked, "How about it when I don't understand at all?" Chao-chou answered, "I don't understand even more so." Chao-chou would sometimes have these dialogues that resembled a competition—who could beat the other at being the most empty-headed. Here the monk stood his ground and said to Chao-chou, "Well, do you know that or not?" Chao-chou replied, "I'm not wooden headed. What is it that I don't know?" The monk said, "That's a fine not understanding!" Chao-chou then clapped his hands and left. The adepts of this period often playfully stressed the attitude of not knowing and not understanding—an essential point in practice.

On one occasion, Shih-t'ou told Yao-shan, "Speech and action have nothing to do with it," to which Yao-shan responded, "Not speaking and not acting also have nothing to do with it." In fact, it was after this interchange that Shih-t'ou approved of Yao-shan's practice and realization. Upon this approval, Yao-shan traveled to Yao-shan mountain and began to teach.

We can get a view of his teaching style from dialogues between him and his students. When a monk asked him, "How can one not be confused by the many phenomena?" Yao-shan said, "If you go along with them, how can they obstruct you?" The monk told him that he did not understand. Yao-shan asked, "What phenomena are confusing you?" That was all. How can one not be confused by the ten thousand phenomena, that is, everything in the world you encounter moment by moment? Well, if you just go along with them, there is no problem.

If you don't understand, find the phenomenon that is confusing you right now. That is the point, to continually look into the question, How am I obscuring my clarity just now?

On another occasion, a monk asked Yao-shan, "What is nirvana?" Yao-shan answered, "What did you call it before you opened your mouth?" Such interchanges exemplify Yao-shan's style of teaching.

When Yao-shan was about to die, he yelled out, "The dharma hall is collapsing! Everybody prop it up." Then he looked at all his disciples and said, "None of you understand my meaning." Then—he died.

Now we return to the case itself. It begins with a monk saying, "On a level field, in the shallow grass, the elk and deer form a herd." This is one of those kong-ans that uses one image to talk about something else. This monk is not really interested in fields and grass, deer and elk; he is using these objects to talk about mind and practice. "Level field" is an image of equanimity. In formal practice, one of the prerequisites is to establish a certain degree of equanimity and evenness when you sit, and for that matter, the same is true in the action meditation of daily life. You need the quality of equanimity as a support for clear perception and insight. Suzuki Roshi, using a similar image, says that if you want to control a cow or sheep you should give it a wide open pasture to run in, and you should watch it. That means, if you want to control what is going on in your mind, don't try to get rid of it; instead open to whatever occurs in your mind and just observe it moment by moment.

The next image here is "in the shallow grass." During this era, there was a Zen master named Tan-hsia (Tanka; Dan Ha). Upon becoming a student, he went to call on Ma-tsu. But as soon as Ma-tsu saw him, he said, "Your affinity is not here. Go to Shih-t'ou." Once he arrived, Shih-t'ou sent him to the workman's hall, where he stayed for three years without formally becoming a monk. One day Shih-t'ou announced, "Tomorrow, the whole assembly is going to cut the grass and weeds that are growing in front of the Buddha shrine." The next day, all the monks appeared in front of the Buddha shrine with sickles, hoes, and other tools for cutting grass. But Tan-hsia came carrying a big basin of water. When they had all assembled, Tan-hsia went in front of Shih-t'ou, poured the water over his own head, washed his hair, and bowed down. Shih-t'ou laughed and took out his precepts knife and shaved Tan-hsia's head. As he was beginning to explain the meaning of the various monks' precepts, Tan-hsia covered his ears so as not to hear what Shih-t'ou was saying. Tan-hsia then abruptly returned to Ma-tsu's temple.

In the Zen tradition, sometimes grass and weeds represent attachment and mind complications. When monks or nuns shave their heads and take the precepts, it is called "cutting ignorance grass." On the most obvious level, hair is associated with attachment, because hair has to do with appearance, and we all manifest attachment and clinging on the gross level through appearance and physicality. Once many years ago, my teacher looked at me and said, "You should shave your beard off," testing to see whether I was attached to my beard. I said, "Okay, I can do that. It's no problem. Actually, I grew this beard at someone else's suggestion when I started working as a counselor. That person told me, 'Your face looks too young. No one who comes to you for treatment is going to believe that you know anything. You should grow a beard.'" When my teacher heard that, he said, "Oh, keeping beard is no problem." That means, Who is the beard for? Is it for your own vanity, or does it serve some broader function?

A couple of years ago, I went to China to attend a ceremony at the Temple of the Sixth Patriarch. A big contingent of students was there from a Hong Kong Zen Center. The Zen master of this center is a Chinese nun named Dae Kwan. Most of her students are laypeople. In getting ready for the ceremony, people were putting on their finery: Monks were putting on their ceremonial clothes, and laypeople were getting dressed up. Zen Master Dae Kwan was in a room with a group of her students who were Chinese laywomen. When she saw the kind of preparation they were going through, with their makeup, hair, and clothes, she remembered what it had been like for her when she was a laywoman living in Hong Kong, working in business. She commented, "I was glad I didn't have to do that anymore." On the most obvious level, cutting grass has to do with that kind of thing. We do not realize how much energy we put into keeping up appearances and how much it affects us. But on a more subtle level, cutting grass means cutting off mind obscurations, cutting off clinging tightly to opinions, fixed concepts, and limited ways of seeing things. The image here begins, "On a level field, in the shallow grass [if the grass is shallow, there are not too many complications], the elk and deer form a herd." An old saying goes, "Ten thousand thoughts all become one thought. Ten thousand questions become one question." "The elk and dear form a herd" means that all the divergent energies of your mind come together to one point. Mind becomes stabilized and centered.

The questioning monk does not leave it at that, being satisfied with calm centeredness. He continues, "How can one shoot the elk of elks?" How can one hit the bull's-eye? In meditation practice, it is not enough to just stabilize your mind, calm down, and become quiet. That is necessary and valuable. But ultimately practice is about seeing clearly and seeing into who is the one who is practicing. Who is the master of this level field and shallow grass and the herd converging? Who is that? That is hitting the bull's-eye. My teacher would sometimes say, "A good Zen talk should always leave the student with a question." It should not answer the question; it should leave the student with it. Otherwise it is just somebody else's good idea that the student has swallowed. It has not fully stirred up and mobilized the student's energy potential and gotten to the bull's-eye. How can you shoot the elk of elks?

The essential self has many names. Zen Master Lin-chi (Rinzai) called it the person of no rank and no title. In this case, it is a big title: elk of elks. The Sixth Patriarch referred to it by asking, "What is your original face before your parents were born?" Some Zen Masters call it mind essence; others just refer to it as master. But all these names are pointing to the same thing. So when, in the kong-an, Yao-shan says, "Look—an arrow!" looking is the arrow and the bull's-eye.

The Sufi tradition talks about a wise fool named Nasruddin. One day Nasruddin was out in front of his house, crawling around on all fours. A friend came by and asked, "Nasruddin, what are you doing?" Nasruddin replied, "I am looking for my key." The friend said he would help and got down on the ground and started going through the grass. But neither found anything, even though they were looking for quite a while. Finally the friend said, "Where did you misplace your key?" Nasruddin answered, "In the house." "Then why are we looking out here?" the friend asked. Nasruddin said, "Because out here there's more light." A Zen master commenting on this story said, "Looking is the key." That is the same point made here: Look! An arrow! There is a saying in the Buddhist tradition: Just seeing is buddha nature. Just hearing is enlightenment, just sitting is actualizing your true being, and just having a big question—don't know—is perceiving your mind's essence. So when Yao-shan says, "Look!" he reveals his first arrow. The monk immediately falls down—*ptchh*—as if hit by the arrow.

In the Zen tradition, you find images of life and death used as teaching metaphors pointing toward different aspects of practice. Once when Chao-chou and T'ou-tzu (Tosu; Tu Ja) were talking, Chao-chou said, "How is it when the man of great death returns to life?" T'ou-tzu replied, "Going by night is not permitted. You must arrive in daylight." The phrases "great death" and "returns to life" appear often in Zen terminology.

The same ideas appear in a story about a student of Zen Master Ma-tsu named Shih-kung. He was originally a hunter and did not like Buddhism or monks. However, one day as he was passing Ma-tsu's temple, Ma-tsu asked him, "Are you a hunter?" Shih-kung said that he was. "Do you know how to shoot?" Shih-kung said yes. "Do you know how to shoot the whole herd with one arrow?" Shih-kung did not understand Ma-tsu's intent, so he said, "The herd are living beings; why shoot the whole herd?" Ma-tsu replied, "Then do you know how to shoot yourself?" At that point, Shih-kung put down his bow and arrows and became Ma-tsu's student.

In later years, Shih-kung began to teach. Whenever a student would come, he would pick up his bow and arrow and draw the bow. Few students knew how to respond. But one who did was San-ping. As this student was coming through the door, Shih-kung picked up his bow and drew his arrow. San-ping immediately opened his robes, stuck out his chest, and said, "Is this arrow the arrow that kills or the arrow that gives life?" Shih-kung put the arrow down and strummed the bowstring three times. San-ping bowed to him. After that, Shih-kung broke his bow and arrows and said, "For twenty years I have practiced this way and have only been able to shoot half a person."

San-ping's question—Is this arrow the arrow that kills or the arrow that gives life?—is important in our own practice. If you look at certain aspects of practice, like renunciation, you see processes like giving up ideas, opinions, concepts, and images of self. Giving up the image of a constructed self, with which we identify most of the time, feels like dying. If you can accept that everything is changing moment by moment, this acceptance of change is already renunciation, because you accept that nothing is remaining fixed and permanent. Moment by moment, in some way, we are always losing our balance or dying a small death. That is one side—the arrow that kills.

But by being open to that experience, we also grow and expand: We come to life. On one side there is letting go of the idea of self, and on the other there is being reborn as just seeing, just hearing, just acting, and just experiencing, without idea or image. This is the arrow that gives life.

One day a monk asked Chao-chou, "What is meditation?" Chao-chou answered, "It's not meditation." The monk then asked, "Why is it not meditation?" Chao-chou replied, "Because it's alive!" If we think about meditation, it becomes a very serious affair. But it is not a serious affair. It is alive!

Now back to the case. After the monk fell down, Yao-shan said, "Attendant, drag this dead wretch out." This means that if you are going to stay there lying on the floor, then you only understand one side, and you are not much use to anybody. If you are not going to come alive, then I will come alive by summoning the attendant to drag you out of here. Zen masters sometimes respond to an action like the monk's falling down and staying there by saying, "You understand one, but you don't understand two," or "Your head is a dragon, but your tail is a snake," meaning that you look good at first, but now what? Are you going to just stay there? If you are, you are not utilizing your spiritual potential. You are not using your just seeing, just hearing, just acting, just connecting with this world in some kind of compassionate way. So when Yao-shan told the attendant to drag the dead wretch out, the monk immediately got up and ran out. He got up and came alive.

One commentary says, "He still has some breath left."[2] But running out is not an engaged response. Yao-shan says, "This fool is just playing with a mudball—when will it ever end?"

An old fable relates that a rabbit said to an ostrich, "Don't stick your head in the sand. Run away as I do." But running away is not the full engagement of coming alive and connecting with the situation. It does not manifest the elk or elk's function. Essentially Zen practice is the practice of not running out on ourselves and not running out on this world.

Notes

1. Seung Sahn, trans., *The Blue Cliff Record* (Cumberland, RI: Kwan Um School of Zen, 1983), 62.
2. Thomas Cleary and J. C. Cleary, trans., *The Blue Cliff Record* (Boston: Shambhala, 1992), 444.

CHAPTER 4

National Teacher Chung's Seamless Monument

. . . .

Can true nature be revealed through speech?

Can it be expressed through silence?

Can it be demonstrated through action?

What is the interconnectedness of speech, silence, and action?

Haahh!!

Above, the mountain towers high; in the valley, a big echo.

. . . .

The Blue Cliff Record and *Book of Serenity* include this kong-an as case 18 and case 85, respectively.

Emperor Tsu Tsung asked National Teacher Hui Chung, "After you die, what will you need?"

The National Teacher said, "Build a seamless monument for me."

The Emperor said, "Please, Master, the monument's form?"

The National Teacher was silent for a long time. Then he asked, "Do you understand?"

The emperor said, "I don't understand."

The National Teacher said, "I have a disciple to whom I

have transmitted the teaching, Tan Yuan, who understands this well. Please summon him and ask him about it."

After the National Teacher passed on, the Emperor summoned Tan Yuan and asked him what the meaning of this was. Tan Yuan said, "South of Hsiang, north of T'an."

Hsueh Tou added the comment, "A single hand does not make sound."

"In the middle there is enough gold for a country."

Hsueh Tou added the comment, "A rough-hewn staff."

"No shadow under the tree, the community ship."

Hsueh Tou added the comment, "The sea is calm; the rivers are clear."

"In the crystal palace, nobody understands."

Hseuh Tou added the comment, "Raised up."[1]

Hui-chung (Chu Kokushi; Hae Chung), the national teacher, was a disciple of the Sixth Patriarch who lived to be about one hundred. Because of his association with the Sixth Patriarch, as well as his reputation as a great teacher, he was visited by many. He was born to a peasant family in a small village in the south of China where, it is said, he never spoke nor crossed the bridge in front of his family's house until he was sixteen years old. That was when a Zen master appeared, and the boy immediately crossed the bridge, bowed to the teacher, and said, "Please, master, I want to take refuge in meditation and the Way. Please ordain me as a monk and take me as a student."

The Zen master said, "The teaching of our sect is very steep. If someone who is not worthy of the task takes up the teaching of our sect, then it will decline. So how could you, who are essentially a country bumpkin, be equal to this task?"

The boy replied, "The true teaching is about equality, so why do you make high and low? Why do you hinder my good intentions by talking this way?"

The Zen master studied him for a minute and then said, "If you leave home and become a monk, you shouldn't follow me." The boy asked, "Well then, where should I go to find a good teacher?" The Zen master replied, "You should go to Mount Ts'ao Ch'i in Canton Province. There the Sixth Patriarch is teaching an assembly of six hundred monks. Do you know where that is?" The boy said, "I've never even heard of the place." Yet he set off on the journey and eventually reached the temple of the Sixth Patriarch.

At the time the boy arrived, the Sixth Patriarch was about to give his dharma discourse. The boy immediately approached the Sixth Patriarch and bowed. The patriarch asked, "Where are you coming from?" The boy said, "I've just come here." The Sixth Patriarch asked, "Well, where were you born?" The boy replied, "Since having gotten the five *skandhas*, I don't remember." The patriarch said, "Seriously, tell me, what province are you from?" When the boy told him, the patriarch said, "Why did you come here?" The boy said, "It is difficult to encounter both the dharma and a good teacher, so I came here for that reason. And because I want you to ordain me as a monk and take me as a student." The patriarch tried to put him off, saying, "You shouldn't become a monk. If you stay in the world you will become an emperor." But the boy replied, "What need have I to become an emperor? Please ordain me." At that, the patriarch accepted him as his student.

The boy studied with the patriarch for many years and became one of his successors. After that he went to a small temple on a mountain, where he practiced for forty years. His reputation spread, and eventually the emperor summoned him. He taught in the palace for a number of years before retiring to his mountain. But when the emperor passed away, Hui-chung was recalled by the son who had succeeded his father. By then the national teacher was already quite old, which is why the younger emperor asked him, "When you die what will you need?"

Both emperors took the precepts from the national teacher, and some Zen histories list them among his dharma successors. His main student, however, was Tan-yuan (Tangen; Chim Won), the monk who recites the verse in this story. Tan-yuan and the national teacher appear in another kong-an in the *Wu-men-kuan* (*Mumonkan; Mu Mun Kwan*), which identifies Tan-yuan as the national teacher's attendant. That story recounts:

> The National Teacher called to his attendant three times,
> and the attendant answered three times.

In other words, the attendant was going out the door when the national teacher called out, "Attendant!" But when the attendant turned around and said, "Yes?" the national teacher did not say anything. When the attendant was about to leave again, the national teacher called out, "Attendant!" And the attendant again said, "Yes?" Nothing. And a third time, "Attendant!" "Yes?"

> The National Teacher said, "I thought I had deserted you,
> but originally, you deserted me."[2]

For many years, Tan-yuan, serving as Hui-chung's attendant, received this kind of training.

When the emperor asked, "After you die, what will you need?" the national teacher responded, "Build a seamless monument for me." The word translated here as "monument" also means "pagoda," so we could say, Build me a seamless pagoda.

The pagoda in China, Korea, and Japan serves several purposes. It is usually a four- or eight-sided structure, sometimes made of stone or brick if it is small. Large ones are usually made of wood. Pagodas usually have several stories. The bottom story is the largest, and the subsequent ones decrease in size. Pagodas have sloping roofs of glazed tiles, with eaves on each level. At the very top is a pole with several rings, looking rather like an antenna. In fact, it is an antenna of a particular kind.

One purpose of pagodas is to hold the relics of some great teacher. Relics are found by sifting through the ashes following cremation, looking for *shari*—small, jewel-like crystals supposedly found in the ashes of somebody whose practice has been exceptionally strong.

These crystals are considered to be a condensation of that teacher's spiritual energy. They are saved as objects of veneration.

Each pagoda has a central shaft, inside which the relics may be kept. The shaft's exterior usually displays buddha images. A platform or staircase is traditionally built around the central shaft, so disciples or devotees may circumambulate the shaft as a ritual form of walking meditation, venerating the spiritual relics.

The pagoda is also said to have a geomantic influence—related to a kind of spiritual or esoteric science of geomancy that developed in China. It is usually referred to as wind and water geography, identified by its Chinese name, *feng shui*. According to this view, certain places on the earth are centers of spiritual power, similar to the acupuncture points of the human body. A temple with a pagoda is often located in a place where the geomancy is felt to have this power—usually in a valley between mountains. The temple builders would consult with a geomancer to find a location with the proper configuration of mountains and running water. The names for some different mountain peaks in such configurations are White Tiger, Blue Dragon, and Black Turtle.

The tall pole on top of the pagoda acts as a cosmic aerial to draw universal energy to it. And in some way, the energy is stored in the pagoda until it is distributed.

The pagoda also embodies a certain kind of cosmic symbolism, something like the mandala. Tibetan Buddhism uses mandalas in certain meditation practices. The mandala diagrams are constructed of a series of concentric circles. The pagoda is like a three-dimensional mandala, an architectural representation of universal consciousness or enlightened mind. The relics are placed in a representation of the absolute point, the center of the spiritual universe. The four directions emanate from that central shaft, and each direction is associated with a different buddha who embodies some aspect of enlightened wisdom or enlightened awareness. According to yogic ideas, if someone does walking meditation inside or around a pagoda, the spiritual energy contained in the structure enhances their meditation. In India, structures like these are called *stupas*. The name changed to pagoda when they were introduced into China. But both are connected with practice that focuses universal energy.

The national teacher, however, is not really referring to that sort of structure. He says, "Build a seamless monument." A monument or pagoda is a man-made construction and obviously has seams. "Seamless" might apply to the ecological view of nature—that nature has no seams: One thing flows into the next and into the next, each thing balancing and interacting with every other thing in a wide net of interconnectedness. In Buddhism this ecological view expands beyond natural phenomena like mountains, rivers, and valleys. It also encompasses our belief that all interactions and all experiences in the world are interconnected, in some way always affecting everything else. That is the fundamental meaning of *seamless*.

A verse written by Zen Master Hsueh-tou (Setcho) comes after the case and talks about the seamless monument:

> The seamless monument—
> To see it is hard.
> A clear pool does not admit the blue dragon's coils.
> Layers upon layers.
> Shadows upon shadows—
> For ever and ever it is shown to people.[3]

The poem's second line, "To see it is hard," refers to the emperor asking the national teacher, "Please, Master, the monument's form?" The national teacher just remains silent. The third line mentions a blue dragon, and since the dragon is a symbol of spiritual power in China, this refers to the national teacher's silence. When a dragon is coiled up, it is sleeping, but here the poem says, "A clear pool does not admit the blue dragon's coils," suggesting that the national teacher's silence is not a passive, non-energetic silence, or sleepiness.

The second line suggests that the seamless monument is hard to see. But the last line says, "For ever and ever it is shown to people." So is the seamless monument hard to see or is it always shown to people?

Which is correct? Look deeply and perceive the meaning. If you enter here, then hard to see and easy to see are both transcended.

A monk asked Zen Master Daling of Korea, "What is purity in all places?" Daling replied, "Breaking a branch of jewel, every inch is precious; cutting sandalwood, each bit is fragrant."[4] If you take sandalwood and turn it into incense, it smells fragrant. If you take sandalwood and make a little box out of it, still it smells fragrant. If you take sandalwood and carve a statue out of it, the fragrance remains the same. Even though the form is constantly changing, one thing remains perfectly—and seamlessly—consistent. We might compare that to water in different containers. Put water into a round container, it becomes round; put it into a square container, it becomes square. But no matter what shape the water takes, it never relinquishes its own nature.

Both *The Blue Cliff Record* and *Book of Serenity* include comments to this kong-an, added by Zen masters of later generations. One refers to the first line, where the emperor asks the national teacher, "After you die, what will you need?" The comment in *Book of Serenity* says, "Right now he doesn't lack anything."[5]

That is just like us. Right now we do not lack anything either. This, essentially, is the true spirit of practice: Right now, each and every one of us does not lack anything. Then why practice? That is the paradox of practice. On the one hand, we have an aspiration toward something; at the same time, right in this moment, every one of us is already complete. We do not lack anything. Our aspiration is to get a clear view of that fact: that here and now we do not lack anything. And whether that perception comes as a big lightning bolt or somehow imperceptibly sneaks up on us is not important. What is important is that we gradually stabilize and steady that view more and more. That is true practice. If we try anything else, we wind up striving to become something other than ourselves, which usually ends in disaster.

After the national teacher says, "Build a seamless monument," the emperor asks, "The monument's form?" What will it look like?

Zen Master Wu-tsu (Goso; Oh Jo) added a comment:

> In front it is pearls and agate, in back it is agate and pearls;
> on the east are Avalokitesvara and Mahasthamaprapta, on
> the west are Manjusri and Samantabhadra; in the middle
> there's a flag blown by the wind, saying "Flap, flap."[6]

Avalokiteshvara symbolizes compassion, Manjushri wisdom. But if you attain the "flap, flap" of the windblown flag, all the rest emerges naturally.

When the national teacher sits silently and then says, "Do you understand?" a comment from *Book of Serenity* says, "Here you can't understand; though not understanding, don't seek elsewhere."[7]

Zen practice is having confidence or faith in a mind that is free of knowing. We all feel uncomfortable with that sometimes. Then we try to organize the world of our experience into categories. We label, we begin erecting a structure that lets us feel we are controlling things, ordering them, so we can feel secure. But here it says, "Though not understanding, don't seek elsewhere." Do not erect a fortress securing your ground. Try to stay in the openness of not understanding. Do not seek elsewhere. This is our practice.

When the emperor says, "I don't understand," one commentary suggests, "Now he's getting somewhere."[8] The national teacher's final words are, "I have a disciple to whom I have transmitted the teaching, Tan-yuan, who understands this well. Please summon him and ask him about it." And that is what the emperor eventually did. When Tan-yuan appeared, the emperor told him about the incident and asked about the meaning of the seamless pagoda. Tan-yuan remained silent for a while and then recited his poem. *The Blue Cliff Record* commentary says, "Putting aside [the emperor's] not understanding for the moment, did Tan-yuan understand?"[9] Let us take another look at Tan-yuan's verse:

> South of Hsiang, north of T'an.
> In the middle there is enough gold for a country.
> No shadow under the tree, the community ship.
> In the crystal palace, nobody understands.

"South of Hsiang, north of T'an," is like saying south of Canada, north of Mexico or, conversely, north of Canada, south of Mexico. That means everywhere and nowhere, just as it is in this moment.

A verse written about "South of Hsiang, north of T'an" says:

> The sky is high, earth is wide,
> the sun is to the left, the moon is to the right[10]

That is everywhere and nowhere, just as it is, just now, moment by moment.

Then Tan-yuan's next line, "In the middle there is enough gold for a country," suggests that in that space there are immense riches. Later, Zen Master Tan-hsia (Tanka; Dan Ha) wrote a verse on this line:

> All heaven and earth is the country of gold;
> Myriad beings completely manifest the pure subtle
>   body.[11]

Tan-yuan says the country is full of gold, but Tan-hsia says the country itself is gold. That means that just now our mind, just as it is, is complete. The original body remains clear constantly. Speech, words, ideas, conceptions—nothing can hinder it.

Then the third line says, "No shadow under the tree, the community ship." This line sometimes is translated a little differently: "Under the shadowless tree, the community ferry boat." The shadowless tree is what Zen Master Seung Sahn calls true nature's secret language, true nature's secret words. If you perceive your true nature and hear a phrase like "under the tree, no shadow," you understand what this means, because it points to something unusual and free, something magical. If you perceive your true nature, you feel suddenly like you have been set free. The small, contracted sense of yourself that you had before opens up. Zen language expresses this with terms like "shadowless tree," or "the stone man does a dance," or "the wooden chicken is crowing in the evening." That is true nature's secret language—secret words that point toward the experience of enlightenment.

"Under the shadowless tree, the community ferryboat." That means that enlightenment is not just for me. It is a community ferryboat. The great Zen adept Layman P'ang, commenting on his enlightenment said, "When I'm hungry I eat, when I'm tired I sleep." But "community ferryboat" means, in addition, that if someone else is thirsty, offer them something to drink. Our practice is not just for ourselves but is to be spread widely in some way. This does not necessarily suggest proselytizing, trying to teach everyone to sit Zen meditation, although that is not a bad idea. Somehow the spirit of practice should radiate out and be like a community ferryboat, helping people cross in various ways.

The last line says, "In the crystal palace, nobody understands," or "nobody who knows." It is not that nobody is there, just nobody who understands. The emptiness of bright, shining awareness clearly perceives without recourse to concepts.

An allusion to the seamless pagoda was given to a dharma sister of mine who went to a forest meditation center in Thailand. This center is completely natural in its style, with no amenities of any kind. She said that the first time she went there to practice, she asked the master, "Where is the temple? Where is the beautiful gold statue of the Buddha?" The master simply said, "Buddha is always practicing and teaching in the forest." On the last day of the retreat, when he gave his final talk, the master said, "Do you remember, somebody asked why there is no temple and no Buddha statue? That's because the forest is already a temple, everything is buddha, nature is always speaking the dharma."

My teacher, Zen Master Seung Sahn, went to meet this Thai meditation master, and they immediately formed a warm relationship. Then he was taken to see the Thai master's hut. It was really small, only big enough for one person to sleep in. Seung Sahn looked inside and said, "Oh, it's empty! You have nothing, like a monk!" Then he turned to the master and said, "Your room is very good. My room is very complicated." Later, when they were getting set to leave, Zen Master Seung Sahn said to him, "Your dharma is very high class. My dharma is very low class. No electricity. Very wonderful!"[12]

If we do not get too enamored with the back-to-nature theme, there is an important point in Seung Sahn's comparison: Your room is empty; my room is complicated. "No electricity. Very wonderful!" We all have a tendency to carry many concepts and opinions with us, and these two comments point to the fact that carrying things prevents us from meeting our world just as it is. Similarly we do not meet ourselves just as we are. That is why Zen teaching emphasizes over and over: Put it all down.

We need to put down our bundle of opinions and concepts over and over again. If you carry a bundle, things become complicated. Here it is important to recognize the distinction between complex and complicated. Complexity is a natural phenomenon; the interconnections in this universe are quite complex. But complications are something that we make. We see something and say, Oh, that's complicated. Then we react in response to that label. We bring along a bundle that gets in the way of just seeing what is there.

Zen practice is to just see and act clearly and compassionately, without making mental constructs. If we cultivate that spirit repeatedly, then we are in accord with the national teacher's seamless monument. We honor our obligation to all the great women and men who have passed on this tradition to us. Likewise we are fulfilling our responsibility to all those who come after us and will benefit from this tradition. At the same moment, we are fulfilling our responsibility and obligation to ourselves.

Notes

1. Seung Sahn, trans., *The Blue Cliff Record* (Cumberland, RI: Kwan Um School of Zen, 1983), 15.
2. Seung Sahn, trans., *The Mu Mun Kwan* (Cumberland, RI: Kwan Um School of Zen, 1983), 21.
3. Thomas Cleary and J. C. Cleary, trans., *The Blue Cliff Record* (Boston: Shambhala, 1992), 121.
4. Thomas Cleary, trans., *Book of Serenity* (Boston: Shambhala, 1988), 363.
5. Ibid., 365.
6. Cleary and Cleary, 118.

7. Cleary, 365.

8. Ibid.

9. Cleary and Cleary, 119.

10. Cleary, 365.

11. Ibid., 363.

12. Corrin Chan, "Forest Dharma," *Primary Point* 16, no. 2 (1998): 6.

CHAPTER 5

Nan-ch'uan's Flowering Tree

If you relate to the great matter through understanding,
you will feel like a person who is sleepwalking through
a dream, because understanding alone cannot help you.

If you do not understand, but cling to that point, then you fall
down into the deep pit of emptiness and cannot help anyone,
including yourself.

Going beyond these two, understanding and not understanding,
what is it that becomes clear?

Haahh!!

Spring breeze fills the air. Look! Flowers are all of reds,
blues, and yellows.

Case 40 in *The Blue Cliff Record* states:

As the officer Lu Hsuan was talking with Zen Master
Nan-ch'uan, he remarked, "Master of the teachings Seng
Chao once said, 'Heaven, earth, and I have the same root;
ten thousand things and I are one body.' This is outrageous."
[*Outrageous* here does not have a negative connotation but
rather means "marvelous, incredible, far out."]

Nan-ch'uan pointed to a flower in the garden. He called to the officer and said, "People these days see this flowering tree as a dream."[1]

Zen Master Seung Sahn's commentary on this kong-an says: "Open your mouth, big mistake. Close your mouth, the whole universe and you are never separate. Wake up! wake up! What do you see now? What do you hear now? Go ask the dog and the cat, and they will teach you."[2]

Nan-ch'uan (Nansen; Nam Cheon) (747–834) was one of the very great Zen masters of China during the T'ang Dynasty. He was a student of Zen Master Ma-tsu (Baso; Ma Jo). As a ten-year-old he received instruction from his first teacher, but he did not become fully ordained as a monk until he reached the age of thirty.

Nan-ch'uan first made a detailed study of the teachings connected with the monk's rules, which are quite extensive, and then he traveled around China to different temples, where he studied the various sutra teachings and the philosophy of the Middle Way. Thus by the time he met Zen Master Ma-tsu, he was about forty and already well versed in Buddhism. There is a saying in Korea: If someone is useless to society, they become a monk; and if they are useless as a monk, then they become a Zen monk; and if they are completely rotten as a Zen monk, then they become a Zen master. You could say that Nan-ch'uan followed that sequence! He had scarcely turned forty when he became awakened, under the direction of Zen Master Ma-tsu.

Nan-ch'uan then freed himself of everything he had learned previously. This means he did not cling to any ideas or concepts from all the scriptural and doctrinal teachings that he had embodied. After the death of Ma-tsu in 788, Nan-ch'uan, then forty-one years old, set off on another long pilgrimage, calling on many other Zen masters. Seven years later, he went to the top of Mount Nan-ch'uan and lived in relative seclusion in a small temple for the next thirty years, never coming down from the mountain. Students climbed the mountain to be with him, the most famous being Zen Master Chao-chou (Joshu; Joju).

When Nan-ch'uan was in his late seventies, the military governor, Officer Lu Hsuan (Riku; Yu Kan), entreated him to descend the mountain and teach more widely. So for probably the last five or six years of his life, Nan-ch'uan had a wider following of several hundred students. Lu Hsuan became one of his seventeen successors who became teachers.

This kong-an takes place when Officer Lu Hsuan is still a student. The other person referred to in the kong-an is master of the teachings Chao. This was a monk named Seng Chao (Jo Hosshi; Gae Poep Sa) (378–414), who lived in China much earlier than Nan-ch'uan. In fact, he predates Bodhidharma's arrival in China around 450, and thus the Zen tradition. The highly esteemed Seng Chao was one of the great Kumarajiva's main students. The latter had come from central Asia to China and set up a school and committee to translate all the important sutras and treatises on Buddhism and Buddhist philosophy from Sanskrit into Chinese.

When Dharma Master Chao was young, he studied Taoist teachings, like those of Lao-tzu and Chuang-tzu. But once, as he was copying the Vimalakirti Sutra, he had an awakening. He then felt that Buddhism was more thorough than Taoism, so he became a monk and studied under Kumarajiva. He wrote an important treatise—the one that Officer Lu Hsuan is quoting here in the kong-an.

The essence of Master Chao's teaching is that the myriad phenomena that one encounters are oneself.

The kong-an says that as the officer and Nan-ch'uan were walking in the garden, the officer said, "Master of the teachings Chao once said, 'Heaven, earth, and I have the same root.'" In Taoist philosophy, heaven and earth represent two universal polarities: creativity and receptivity. These two terms were widely used by Chinese people; they are similar to the terms *yin* and *yang*. When, for example, a monk asked Zen Master Chao-chou, "What about a person who has gone beyond heaven and earth?" Chao-chou asserted, "I'm waiting for there to be such a person, to reply to him." That is Chao-chou's subtlety. If he were going to be just a little more confrontational, he would have said, "If you go beyond heaven and earth, then I'll answer you." But he does not even get that much energy up: Just, I'm waiting for such a person to appear, and then I'll reply to him.

In this statement within the kong-an—Heaven and earth and I have the same root—heaven and earth are not as important as root. The question is, What is this root that heaven, earth, and I share identically? What is it that we all share in common? What is the essential root?

The Heart Sutra says, "All dharmas are marked by emptiness." That means all phenomena condition each other and none can subsist on their own. Good makes bad, bad makes good; white conditions black, black conditions white; you reading conditions me writing, my writing conditions your reading. The fact that you are acting as students makes me the Zen master. The fact that I am the teacher defines you as the students. All these pairs are interdependent. So the basic truth of everything is that everything shares in this root of interdependence.

In another place in the same treatise, Master Chao says, "Who can understand that myriad things are his own self."[3] Buddhism speaks a lot about two things—wisdom and compassion. Wisdom is to perceive clearly the truth that we all share in this same root of interdependency. Compassion is the activity of that truth or, as Zen Master Seung Sahn sometimes said, it is enlightenment's job. In Zen you hear a lot about enlightenment. But what is enlightenment's job? Enlightenment's job is compassionate activity.

I know someone who is a hoarder, meaning that he saves things. It's almost like Buddhism: Sentient beings are numberless; we vow to save them all. We recognize the absolute value of each thing, so none is to be discarded. But this person takes this quite literally. If he reads the Sunday *New York Times* and sees an article that might be useful to him in the future, he puts the Sunday *Times* in the corner. If he reads a magazine and sees something that he thinks might be useful in the future, he puts that magazine in a bag and sets it against the wall. This person accumulated so much stuff that his bedroom was filled from floor to ceiling with this accumulation. It got so that there was only a pathway from the door to his bed, as the rest of the room filled up with stuff. We all hoard a little bit, but this was an extreme case.

I once asked him, "What motivates you to hold on to all this stuff?" He replied, "Well, someday I'd like to get a really good filing system going. Then I'd cut out all these articles that appear useful to me and file them. Then, if I need to access any information, I'd pull it out of the files. I wouldn't have to depend on anyone else."

So you can see that the heart of the fantasy is total self-sufficiency—you could say, the myth of self-sufficiency. Because, in fact, if you perceive that all things are interdependent, and that all things support and condition one another, and that my existence is actually part of your existence, and your existence is part of my existence, then self-sufficiency is a myth.

We are always dependent in some way. This person who hoards has difficulty accepting any recognition of dependency, so he has devised a huge fortress of stuff that is going to rescue him from interdependence. In the process, he doesn't want to let go of anything, so he has a big problem.

Some people approach meditation in a similar way, with the attitude that through practice they can get rid of all needs and desires. It is a fantasy of invincibility. But, in fact, correct practice is really about what is my correct relationship to the particular situation I find myself in, moment to moment?

One more sentence of Dharma Master Chao's treatise says, "The ultimate man is empty and hollow, without form; yet none of the myriad things are not his own doing."[4] That statement is about participation. If there is a war going on in the world, if there is sadness abroad, I participate in that. I am concerned, rather than regarding it as having nothing to do with me. Likewise, if someone is quite prosperous or successful or joyful, that also is my doing. I participate in that. And that is connected with the first statement in the kong-an: Heaven, earth, and I have the same root.

Then the officer quotes one more sentence: "Ten thousand things and I are one body." What kind of body is that? In the Hua Yen (Avatamsaka) Sutra, there is a metaphoric representation of this teaching. At one point in the sutra, we are introduced to the Buddha's mother, Queen Maya. She describes what it was like to conceive the

Buddha inside her body, saying that at that time the future Buddha was dwelling in the Tushita heaven. Just at the time of conception, she looked toward the Tushita heaven, and some mystic rays from this great bodhisattva, the future Buddha, came down and entered her body. And at that moment, she said, "My body outreached all worlds, and my belly became as vast as space, and yet did not go beyond the human physical size."[5]

How is it possible that the body becomes as vast as space but simultaneously never goes beyond the human physical size?

Zen Master Seung Sahn sometimes taught a meditation practice called dan-tian breathing. *Dan-tian* (hara; tan jan) means "garden of energy." It refers to the spot just below the navel. If you keep your mind gently at that spot and feel the breath at that point, either by slowing down the breath or just perceiving your natural breath there, the energy connected with thinking comes down to that spot. Then the energy connected with feeling comes down there, and then that point expands, bigger, bigger, bigger . . . until *BOOM!* You and the universe become one!

That's something like Queen Maya's conception of the baby Buddha. She goes further, saying, "And as soon as those light rays of the enlightening being had entered my body, I saw all the enlightening beings whose birth-miracles were shown in the spheres at the front of the enlightening being's light rays, as they sat on the Buddha's lion throne at the site of enlightenment, surrounded by congregations of enlightening beings, honored by the leaders of the worlds, turning the wheel of the teaching . . . Yet even though it took in all those multitudes, my belly was not enlarged, nor did this body of mine become any more than a human body."[6]

That is an important point. It means that if you want to attain something, it is not somewhere else. Look into your own body and mind. There maybe you will also find millions of gazillions of bodhisattvas walking around. But if you don't, that is not too important. What is important is to perceive that inside and outside are not separate. That is "ten thousand things and I are one body."

Up to this point, as wonderful as all this is, it does not go beyond doctrinal teaching. You can say it is theoretical Zen.

There is an old saying: Golden chains still bind and gold dust in the eyes still blinds. What is valuable becomes an impediment if you become too attached to it. Conversely, if you are too idealistic, then you miss the value of what is right before you. Doctrine is still in the realm of ideas and concepts and what is known. A monk asked Zen Master Chao-chou, "What is the one road that cuts right through?" "Cuts right through" means cuts through illusion, cuts through delusion, similar to the second bodhisattva vow: "Delusions are endless; I vow to cut through them all."

Chao-chou responded, "Has the boat from Wai Nan arrived yet?" The monk said, "I don't know." Chao-chou said, "Good, it's arrived." That means, at the moment you arrive at don't-know, you have passed beyond doctrine and cut right through—through all illusory ideas.

Getting back to the case, after he quotes the lines from Dharma Master Chao, Officer Lu Hsuan says, "Marvelous, incredible, outrageous. What a teaching!" And Nan-ch'uan, being extremely subtle, just says, while pointing to a flower in the garden, "People these days see this flowering tree as a dream."

If you are cut by a big hunting knife, you know it immediately. But if you are cut by a razor blade, sometimes you don't even realize you have a gash a mile wide and are bleeding to death. Nan-ch'uan's subtlety is like a razor. One commentator[7] said that Nan-ch'uan takes him to the edge of a cliff and pushes him over at that point: "People these days see this flowering tree as a dream."

A few other kong-ans make the same point. One tells how Kuei-shan (Isan; Wi Sahn) had just awakened one morning and was still abed when his number-one disciple, Yang-shan (Kyozan; An Sahn), entered his room. Kuei-shan said to Yang-shan, "I just had a dream. Would you interpret it for me?" Yang-shan took a basin of water and a towel and handed them to Kuei-shan. Then his second disciple, Hsiang-yen (Kyogen; Hyang Om), came in, and Kuei-shan said to him, "I just had a dream and your brother Yang-shan interpreted it for me. Can you also interpret it for me?" Hsiang-yen, seeing that Kuei-shan already had the basin with the towel, handed him a cup of tea. Kuei-shan was not looking for dream interpretation but rather for correct action in the moment. He was testing his two students. When you wake up, then what? Wash your face and have a cup of tea.

Zen Master Seung Sahn writes in one of his poems:

Guest and host exchanging last night's dream:
Who will tell these two they are in a dream?[8]

Later Yang-shan had his own dream, which forms one of the kong-ans in the *Wu-men-kuan*. It says that Yang-shan had a dream, and in the dream he went to Maitreya's heaven. There, in the assembly in Maitreya's heaven, he was given the third seat, which is a highly respected seat. Then a monk hit the gavel and announced, "Today the dharma speech will be given by the monk in the third seat." So Yang-shan mounted the rostrum, hit the gavel, and proclaimed, "The dharma of the Mahayana goes beyond the four propositions and the hundred negations. Listen carefully, listen carefully." The four propositions and the hundred negations represent Buddhist philosophy. But Yang-shan said, "The dharma of the Mahayana goes beyond the four propositions and the hundred negations," adding, "Listen carefully, listen carefully." Even in his dream he proclaims, "Listen carefully"

In the Lotus Sutra, a parable tells of a poor man who goes to visit his wealthy friend. The friend has prepared a banquet. They sit and eat and drink a lot of alcohol. The poor man, quite drunk and full, goes to sleep. The rich friend has to leave on business but does not want to wake the poor friend. He also wants to give him something to help him with his condition and plight. So, before leaving him, he sews a precious gem into the lining of the poor man's robe.

When the poor man wakes from his drunken stupor and realizes that his friend has left, he leaves the house to resume his travels. He continues to have a hard time, eking out a living by hiring himself out in various places for food and lodging. He barely exists.

When the rich man encounters his poor friend again and perceives his pitiful condition, he asks him, "How could you be so foolish as to continue existing like this? Don't you know that at our last meeting I sewed a precious gem into your robe?" He then reaches into the lining of the poor man's robe, takes out the precious gem, and gives it to him.

We all live in a dream like that, and our dream is composed of our self-limiting and self-defining concepts. We all could awaken to the fact that we already possess something that is far beyond the limiting ideas we hold of ourselves and each other. We could awaken by recognizing that we already have everything. It is not something we are going to make or discover out there; it is already within us. We need to recognize that and respect its value and share it widely in this world. Then change is possible.

Notes

1. See Seung Sahn, *The Whole World Is a Single Flower* (Rutland, VT: Tuttle, 1992), 209.
2. Ibid.
3. Thomas Cleary and J. C. Cleary, trans., *The Blue Cliff Record* (Boston: Shambhala, 1992), 245.
4. Ibid.
5. Thomas Cleary, trans., *The Flower Ornament Scripture: A Translation of the Avatamsaka Sutra*, vol. 3 (Boston: Shambhala, 1987), 312.
6. Ibid., 312–13.
7. See Cleary & Cleary, 246.
8. Seung Sahn, *Bones of Space* (Cumberland, RI: Primary Point Press, 1982), 10.

CHAPTER 6

Te-shan Carrying His Bundle

If you attain the fundamental point, then you perceive
the meaning of a pure white cow on open clear ground.

If you don't stay here but move beyond this scene, then you perceive
the meaning of a relaxed old cow, who lies in the grass and chews its cud.

Going beyond these two, you arrive at a realm where concepts
like form and emptiness have no meaning and subject and object
are no longer a hindrance.

But what is the meaning?

Haahh!!

If someone is thirsty, take them to the kitchen and kindly offer
them a glass of milk.

Case 4 in *The Blue Cliff Record* is entitled, "Te-shan Carrying His Bundle." The story says:

When Te Shan arrived to visit Kuei Shan, he carried his
bundle with him into the dharma room, where he crossed
from east to west and from west to east. He looked around
and said, "There's nothing, nothing." Then he went out.
    Hsueh Tou added the comment, "Completely exposed."

But when Te Shan got to the monastery gate, he said, "I shouldn't have been so brash." So he composed himself properly to meet Kuei Shan. As Kuei Shan sat there, Te-shan held up his sitting mat and said, "Master!"

Kuei Shan reached for his whisk.

Then Te Shan shouted Katz!, whirled with his sleeves trailing, and left.

Hsueh Tou added the comment, "Completely exposed."

Te Shan turned his back on the dharma room, put on his grass shoes, and left.

That evening, Kuei Shan asked the head monk, "Where is that newcomer who just came?"

The head monk answered, "At that time he turned his back on the dharma room, put on his grass shoes, and left."

Kuei Shan said, "Hereafter that lad will go to the summit of a solitary peak, build himself a grass hut, and go on cursing the Buddhas and slandering the Patriarchs."

Hsueh Tou added the comment, "Adding frost on the snow."[1]

A teaching of Zen Master Fo-yan relates to this case. He called it the two diseases. The first disease is to ride an ass in search of an ass. You look for something outside yourself that you already have near at hand, that you are already at one with. That's a very important point, or attitude, in terms of Zen practice—formal meditation practice and even informal meditation-in-action practice. If you practice sitting meditation with an attitude that you want to become something other than what you already are, that is a disease. But if you sit just to wake up to the fact that you are already complete, then your practice direction is clear. So that is the first disease, to ride an ass in search of an ass.

The second disease is to ride an ass and refuse to dismount. In this case, you're clear about what you've got under you, what you're at one with. You've already perceived or attained some degree of stillness and have entered into this fundamental point, but you've become attached to that, and in that attachment you've begun to lose your way. That's what he means by the second disease. Fo-yan then stated the final attitude or correct direction: Do not ride at all. That means you are already the ass. The whole world is also the ass. The whole world then becomes your playground or the manifestation of the field of practice, everywhere in everything at all times.

There are two characters here: Zen Master Kuei-shan (Isan; Wi Sahn) and Zen Master Te-shan (Tokusan; Dok Sahn). Kuei-shan (771–853) began to study the sutras as well as the texts connected with a monk's discipline when he entered a monastery at age fifteen. But then, when he was about twenty-three years old, he felt that this direction was not getting him where he wanted to go. So upon hearing about Zen Master Pai-chang (Hyakujo; Baek Jang), he made a journey to meet him. Pai-chang perceived Kuei-shan as a good vessel and accepted him as his student.

One night, when Kuei-shan was attending the master, Pai-chang asked, "Who are you?" Kuei-shan replied, "I'm Kuei-shan." Then Pai-chang said, "Poke the firepot and see if there's a bit of live charcoal in there." Kuei-shan went to the firebox and took a poker or tongs and poked around but couldn't find a glowing ember, so he said to Pai-chang, "The fire is completely out." You may realize that Pai-chang was not talking about charcoal and fire here, but Kuei-shan did not consciously recognize that his teacher was trying to point him toward his own fundamental aliveness.

Pai-chang then stood up, dug deep in the firepot, pulled out a small piece of glowing charcoal, and held it up in front of Kuei-shan and said, "Is this not it?" (Some translations say, "Just this, you see?") And at that moment—*ptchh*—Kuei-shan had a realization.

Kuei-shan was then in his mid-twenties and, after this experience, having realized some live fire within himself, nevertheless he stayed on at Pai-chang's monastery for another twenty years. That's an important point in terms of one's attitude toward practice, sincerity, and not being in a hurry. In Pai-chang's monastery, Kuei-shan served as head cook, or rice steward, a highly responsible job.

When Kuei-shan was in his forties, a diviner came to the monastery and said to Pai-chang, "If you were to establish a monastery on Mount Kuei, that would be a very good practice place, and many people would come and attain to the Zen dharma. But that practice place on the high peak of Mount Kuei is not suitable for you yourself Zen Master, so you should pick somebody else to go."[2] Everybody thought that the head monk would get the job. And the head monk himself thought that he was entitled to the position.

Pai-chang said to the assembly, "Anyone who can pass the test will become the abbot of Kuei-shan." He took a urine bottle and set it down on the floor saying, "This is not a urine bottle. What then can you call it?" The head monk stepped forward and said, "It can't be called a wooden block."

Then Kuei-shan came forward and—*plaff!*—kicked over the urine bottle and walked out. Pai-chang said, "The head monk has been defeated by Kuei-shan." Kuei-shan would become the abbot of the monastery.

In his mid-to-late forties, Kuei-shan went to Mount Kuei, but he didn't build a temple there. He didn't gather any students around himself, nor did he teach anything. He just built a little hut, nothing spectacular, nothing to grab anyone's attention, and just practiced for seven or eight years. Gradually the sincerity and energy of his practice drew people to him, and a congregation developed around him. Then a government official donated money to build a temple. Kuei-shan eventually had a community of over fifteen hundred monks.

Much later, when Kuei-shan had grown old, he said to his assembly, "When I die, I will be reborn as a cow, at the foot of Mount Kuei. And you will see on the side of this cow, if you look closely, the Chinese characters that say, 'This is the monk Kuei-shan.' But if you call me Kuei-shan, you will miss the cow. On the other hand, if you call me a cow, you will miss Kuei-shan. What then is my correct name?"

If you find that name, even now you can meet Kuei-shan, eyebrow-to-eyebrow.

Te-shan was originally a teaching monk, well-versed in the Diamond Sutra. When he heard about Zen monks in the south of China who weren't studying the sutras but were just sitting facing the wall and claiming to get enlightenment, he decided he would go to the south and teach them the correct way. Te-shan had a rather fiery spirit and a very strong intention.

In the south of China, he met Zen Master Lung-t'an (Ryutan; Yong Dam). One night he stayed up talking to Lung-t'an until Lung-t'an said, "It's late. You should retire." Te-shan started to go to his room, but it was pitch dark outside. He came back in and said to Lung-t'an, "It's dark outside." Lung-t'an lit a rice paper candle and handed it to him. As Te-shan stood in the doorway, pulling back the curtain to go out, Lung-t'an suddenly—*ptchh*—blew the candle out, and at that moment Te-shan was greatly awakened. The next day he burned all his commentaries on the Diamond Sutra in front of the assembly.

It is some time after this experience that we encounter him in the current case. All fired up with his newfound freedom and enlightenment, he had been traveling around China, calling on various Zen masters, and he heard about Kuei-shan's community.

Before the actual kong-an, an introduction by Zen Master Yuan-wu (Engo) says, "Under the blue sky, in the bright sunlight, you don't have to point out this and that anymore; but the causal conditions of time and season still require you to give the medicine in accordance with the disease. But tell me, is it better to let go, or is it better to hold still?"[3]

This is a question that Zen students are always struggling with. Should I make a strong effort and direct myself toward one point like a great samurai warrior? Or should I release and open up and just let be? Here Yuan-wu says the medicine has to fit the particular situation in the moment.

The first paragraph of the kong-an is very interesting.

> When Te Shan arrived to visit Kuei Shan, he carried
> his bundle with him into the dharma room, where he
> crossed from east to west and from west to east.
> He looked around and said, "There's nothing, nothing."
> Then he went out.

Hsueh-tou, who was the commentator and organizer of these stories, writes a short comment, saying, "Completely exposed."

The first point is Te-shan carrying his bundle into the dharma room. In fact, that is the title of the case. Today we might say he brought an awful lot of baggage with him. In China around 700 or 800, they already understood this psychological attitude.

At that time, monks usually adhered to a certain formality, although occasionally some wild and free spirit might ignore it. The custom was that when you came to a new temple, you would put on your ceremonial robe, enter the main dharma room, spread out your sitting mat, and bow to the abbot or the master of the temple. But here, Te-shan comes into the dharma room still carrying his pack from the road, his bundle. Then he walks from east to west, from west to east, proclaims, "There is nothing, nothing," and walks out. By holding on to his bundle, it appears that he is clinging to something. Some hindering attitude is preventing him from connecting with his situation.

Of course, we all find ourselves frequently carrying some bundle along with us. Either we are making ourselves too exalted, or we are belittling ourselves too much. We are carrying some coloring attitude toward self and the world we encounter, and it obscures what is clear and present. A well-known Zen phrase is, "Put it all down." But if you're going to put it all down, then you first have to perceive what you are carrying. What is it that I am coloring everything with? What kind of attitude is getting in the way? Is it negative? Is it positive? If you perceive that, then you can put it down. Sometimes you have to put it down many, many times. Ultimately you even have to put down the putting down.

Te-shan is carrying a big nothing bundle with him. Nothing, nothing—he's got plenty of nothing.

Sometimes the image of carrying a bundle implies the attitude of obligation. Te-shan seems to feel a compelling obligation to walk in and proclaim, "Nothing, nothing" and wake everybody to that fact. Christianity has an injunction, "Take up the cross, and follow me."[4]

That's a statement of practice obligation. One Zen master said, It's as if our true self wants us to do that, wants us to become clear.

At the Buddhist precepts ceremony, we make the request of ourselves, "May we cast off our obligations and involvements and enter into the uncreated, and by so doing fulfill our greatest obligation." This phraseology comes from a Buddhist monk's or nun's renouncement of worldly affairs in order to realize their (and our) spiritual being. But the notion of the homeless life, or the monk's life, is not limited to monks, because each of us has an obligation to wake up to our true being and our true self. That becomes—if you are a Zen student and practicing the Zen way—your central obligation, to wake up. In so doing, you enter the nonattachment path. When we practice the path of nonattachment, at that moment we are not carrying a bundle. We are not clinging to anything. We are not holding on to any concept or idea.

In Zen there is another familiar image of someone carrying a bundle. This one is quite different from Te-shan's bundle. This character holding a bag, often depicted in Zen brush paintings, goes by the name of Pu-tai. He is usually pictured as a chubby guy with a big round belly who is laughing or smiling. He is often surrounded by a group of children, and he is reaching into his sack to dispense gifts to the children. In China, Pu-tai is considered to be an incarnation of the Buddha of Loving Kindness, Maitreya. So carrying something in a self-centered way is transmuted into carrying something in a selfless, generous, and compassionate way.

Several hundred years ago in Korea, there lived a monk who had a very sincere practice spirit. The people in his village looked up to him and admired him. Whenever they needed a ceremony performed, they would call on this monk, knowing that, because of his purity and sincerity, the ceremony would have great merit to it. At first he would be given the small customary donation for his services. But little by little he began to ask for larger and larger donations from the people, until he started to appear not very sincere and not very pure of heart but quite greedy. The villagers began to say disparagingly that he was making his living from the *moktak*. The moktak is the wooden instrument monks use to accompany their chanting. But the monk seemed impervious to the criticism. He just kept asking for bigger and bigger donations and socking away the money.

Then a big flood came and destroyed many homes in the village, washed away the crops. It was a bad time for everyone. One day the monk appeared in the center of the village with a cart and a big chest. He opened up the chest and began to dispense money to everyone according to their need. So sometimes what might appear to be avariciousness or miserliness is not.

In the commentary to this case, after Te-shan walks into the dharma room and proclaims "There is nothing, nothing" and walks out, the commentator writes, "He has a lot of Ch'an [Zen], but what for?"[5] That means that his spirit and energy are quite strong, but has his wisdom ripened enough for him to really know what to do with it?

There is another point here: He walks into the dharma room carrying his bundle. Besides the formal dharma room, the place of practice, there is the original dharma room—the space of truth. *Dharma* means "truth," or "true way." We all have that space of truth from the beginning. That space is pure and clear and includes relative and absolute. It includes all phenomena and noumena and the perception that each thing is already complete.

There is essentially no coming into or going out of that space, and also no staying there. There is no coming, no going, and no staying, because terms like *coming*, *going*, and *staying* all are relative terms, and in this fundamental space of truth, there is no one thing relative to another. Each thing is just as it is. But if you carry a bundle of some kind into that space and parade it back and forth from east to west and west to east, then that space, which is originally wide and open and clear, begins to become very, very narrow. Thus our practice is to perceive when and how we are doing that and just let go of it, put it down.

At that point, Hsueh-tou comments, "Completely exposed." What is it that is completely exposed? That kind of comment is sometimes called a phrase that comes down on both sides, like a double-edged sword; it cuts both ways. On one side, Te-shan reveals the fundamental point: nothing, nothing. But simultaneously he also reveals where he is stuck. Someone might say to him, If there's nothing, then how do you even open your mouth to say "nothing"? So "completely exposed" means he shows, at that moment, just where he is and where he is not.

Then the next part of the story says, "When Te-shan got to the monastery gate, he said, 'I shouldn't have been so brash.' So he composed himself properly to meet Kuei-shan," which means he put on his ceremonial vestments and came back into the dharma room.

Kuei-shan sat in place.

That's a very interesting image. It's the manifestation of not-moving mind. There is a lot of commotion going on: east to west, west to east, nothing, nothing, going out, coming back with a new set of clothes on. But Kuei-shan, being the old cow that he is, sits in place, just watching.

Sometimes in Zen we talk about host and guest. A guest is that which is coming and going. A host is that which is never moving. In the Lin-chi (Rinzai) tradition—one of the main schools of Zen in China shortly after this time—Zen Master Lin-chi would often use the teaching device of host and guest. The host-and-guest meditational attitude means that you hold the position, as Kuei-shan does, of just perceiving what is coming and going, coming and going, coming and going. Thinking appears; thinking disappears. Sensation appears; sensation disappears. Emotion appears; emotion disappears. You just perceive, sitting there quietly, like an old cow lying in the grass chewing its cud. There may be a big commotion going on, but you don't care. You don't try to get rid of it; you don't try to push it away. Kuei-shan doesn't call out to the attendant, "Carry this lunatic out of here and show him the gate!" You don't try to push anything away.

On the other hand, you don't get caught by it. You just perceive coming and going, coming and going. Fundamentally host and guest are not two separate things. They are like waves and water. The waves are moving, moving, moving. The water is always there. But you can't talk about waves as something separate from the water or water as something separate from waves. If there is water, there are waves. If there is mind, there will be thoughts. So don't be bothered by your thinking when you practice.

Te-shan reenters to meet Kuei-shan, and Kuei-shan just sits there. Then Te-shan holds up his sitting mat and says, "Master!" Monks used to carry some kind of mat or cloth with them so when they came in front of the teacher they could make a formal prostration. But here Te-shan doesn't make the formal prostration but instead holds up the mat. Then he yells out, "Master!"

Kuei-shan just reaches for his whisk and casually raises it—not a very dramatic response to Te-shan. At that time in China, Zen masters would have a horsehair whisk that was an emblem of their position. The whisk would usually be at the side of the seat. Then Te-shan shouts "Katz!" to take away everything again, whirls around, and leaves.

Hsueh-tou comments a second time, "Completely exposed." What is completely exposed there? Has Kuei-shan completely exposed Te-shan? Has Te-shan completely exposed Kuei-shan? Has Hsueh-tou, the commentator, completely exposed both of them? And what is being exposed? Host and guest, coming and going, and not moving?

Then the story says that Te-shan turns his back on the dharma room, puts on his grass shoes, and leaves.

The commentary says, "Te Shan won the hat on his head but lost the shoes on his feet."[6] Now, if you're going to make a long journey, you need both a hat on your head—especially if you're a monk and your head is shaved—but probably more importantly you need the shoes on your feet, which are not as obvious as the hat on your head. It says he won the hat on his head, which means he looked pretty good, but Kuei-shan very quietly took away his shoes.

Kuei-shan still doesn't make much of a commotion, but later he asks the head monk, "Where is that newcomer who just came?" The head monk answers, "At that time, when the two of you got into all this, he turned his back on the dharma room, put on his grass shoes, and left."

So Kuei-shan says, summing up the whole business, "Hereafter that lad will go to the summit of a solitary peak, build himself a grass hut, and go on cursing the Buddhas and slandering the Patriarchs." That means that even though he's way up high somewhere, he has essentially lost his way.

Hsueh-tou adds one more comment: "Adding frost on the snow."[9] You don't need to add frost on top of snow, it is already there, so the comment means, Isn't it obvious?

After the case, there's a poem.

> One "completely exposed"
> A second "completely exposed"
> "Adding frost to snow"—(Te-shan) has had a dangerous fall.
> The General of the Flying Cavalry enters the enemy
> camp;
> How many could regain their safety?
> (Te Shan) hurriedly runs past—
> (But Kuei Shan) doesn't let him go.
> On the summit of a solitary peak, he sits among the
> weeds;
> Bah![7]

The penultimate line is also translated as, "Alas! He is seated among the weeds / On the isolated mountaintop."[8] In Zen poetry, weeds are usually an image of complications and of being all caught up in something. So even though he has gone to an isolated mountaintop, Te-shan is still not free.

Zen practice is to attain the mountaintop and return to the valley. One side is the absolute point. The other side is, just now, how can I help you?

We hope that we will put down our bundles over and over again, untie ourselves from the weeds that we get caught in, and practice the way of openness and compassion.

Notes

1. See Seung Sahn, trans., *The Blue Cliff Record* (Cumberland, RI: Kwan Um School

of Zen, 1983), 4.

2. Actually, Kuei-shan was not Kuei-shan's real name. That was his Zen master's name, which was taken from the mountain on which he eventually built his temple. *Shan* means "mountain" in Chinese, so his name means "Mount Kuei."

3. Thomas Cleary and J. C. Cleary, trans., *The Blue Cliff Record* (Boston: Shambhala, 1992), 22.

4. Mark 10:21.

5. Cleary and Cleary, 23.

6. Ibid.

7. Ibid., 27–28

8. Katsuki Sekida, trans., *Two Zen Classics: Mumonkan and Hekiganroku* (New York: Weatherhill, 1977), 155.

CHAPTER 7

Yang-shan Asks San-sheng, "What Is Your Name?"

If you call a Zen master's staff a stick, then you are attached to its name and its form. If you live from that point of view, then names and forms become a hindrance, and you can't see the living, vital world that is right in front of you.

If you say it is not a stick, then you are attached to negation, and you fall into a world of sterile emptiness and become trapped in the dungeon of nirvana.

Is it a stick or not?

Whack! Whack!

Wake up. Stay awake.

Case 68 in *The Blue Cliff Record* is an interchange called "Yang-shan Asks San-sheng, 'What Is Your Name?'"

In chapter 6, we met Yang-shan's teacher, Kuei-shan. Yang-shan (Kyozan; An Sahn) spent about fifteen years studying with Kuei-shan (Isan; Wi Sahn). The Kuei-yang school, which became the first of five great Chinese teaching traditions, emerged from their combined teaching around the year 800. When Yang-shan was about fifteen years old, he asked his parents' permission to become a monk, but they refused. He agonized over this until two years later when, we are told, he cut off two of his fingers and presented them to his parents as a sign of his sincerity. His parents relented and gave their permission for him to become a monk.

Yang-shan traveled widely, calling on many teachers. With Master Tan-yuan (Tangen; Chim Won) he had an initial awakening. He deepened his experience and understanding at the assembly of Zen Master Kuei-shan, with whom he remained for fifteen years. He then went out and taught on his own.

The teaching style of the Kuei-yang school is called substance and function. In order to understand this style, you might picture a circle with two sides, something like a yin-yang diagram. There is a substance and a function, but even though we talk about them differently, they are essentially not separate.

Substance refers to something that is unnameable—that is, before we attach any ideas, names, forms, words, or speech to it. Sometimes it is represented by a gesture, such as hitting the floor, sometimes by complete silence, because there is nothing that can be said about the essential substance of all things. But this essential substance expresses itself in the world, moment by moment, through various kinds of functions. So the dynamic expression of substance is seen in activity. These two are not separate. If you look at the candle flame and the light that it is radiating, the flame would be the substance, and the illumination would be the function. But it does not make sense to talk about the flame without its light or the light without a flame to radiate it.

In the Kuei-yang school, many stories tell of of interchanges between Kuei-shan, the teacher, and Yang-shan, the student, that demonstrate this style of teaching in a concrete and sometimes comical form. For example, one day Kuei-shan asked Yang-shan, "Where are you coming from?" It was not that he did not know where Yang-shan was coming from at that moment, but he took the opportunity to question him. Yang-shan replied, "From the fields."

Now that is an ordinary kind of answer. Perhaps he was answering in just the common, everyday way and did not get the fundamental point of Kuei-shan's question: Where does your functioning come from, moment by moment? Yang-shan just said, "From the fields." Or maybe he was a highly adept Zen student who recognized that ordinary mind is not separate from the essential point of truth. So he answered casually, in the ordinary way, "From the fields."

Then Kuei-shan pushed him a little by asking, "How many people were there in the fields?" That means, when you were in the fields, were you relating to your experience by making a separation between you and other people, or were you completely unified with the world you were in? Yang-shan immediately took his hoe, shoved it into the ground, folded his hands, and stood silently. How many is that? In reply to this gesture, which had no words, no speech attached to it, Kuei-shan said, "Today there are many people cutting thatch on South Mountain," meaning, if you have revealed this point, then I will return to the everyday mind point myself. At that, Yang-shan took his hoe out of the ground, put it over his shoulder, and walked away. The dialogue was over.

That is a play between the two of them about substance and function and keeping clear about those two. Kuei-shan taught, "The noumenal ground of reality does not admit a single particle, but the methodology of myriad practices does not abandon anything."[1] The true essence does not admit even a single particle of separation; everything is one, and that one is empty of name and form. But at the same time, the methodology of myriad practices does not abandon anything. This means if you are going to practice living from this point of view, then everything in front of you has value; everything is your practice, everything is teaching to you, nothing is to be discarded. Myriad phenomena all have value.

Kuei-shan continued, saying, "If you penetrate directly, then the sense of the ordinary and the sacred disappears, concretely revealing the true constant, where principle and fact are not separate. This is the Buddhahood of being as is."[2] If you can penetrate this matter directly, then all distinctions, such as ordinary and sacred, return to the original mind. And then concretely—not as some lofty idea or philosophy—right in front of you is revealed the true constant of the truth. This is called the buddhahood of being as it is, not something special.

A teaching that comes out of this school and many other Zen traditions says this world is made by thinking. My teacher used to say, "The sky never says, I'm the sky. The grass never says, I'm the grass." We make the names and stick them onto things.

Once a monk approached Korean Zen Master Man Gong and asked, "Where is the Buddha's teaching?" Man Gong replied, "Right in front of you." The monk said, "You say, right in front of you, master, but I don't see it." Man Gong replied, "You construct I, so you don't see it." The monk said, "Do you see it, master?" Man Gong said, "If you make I, it's difficult to see it. But if you make you, it's even more difficult to see it."

We are making some constructed sense of I and some constructed sense of you all the time. What kind of I do I make just now, what kind of you? Practice in the world is perceiving that process, over and over again. First we make I and you, then we begin to adorn them: I'm a failure; you're a success. Or I'm a success; you're a failure. I'm beautiful; you're not so beautiful. Or I'm not so beautiful; but you are very beautiful. I'm good; you're not so good. This is putting clothes on I and you, then taking the labeling very seriously.

Usually some sticky feelings are attached to all those labels. Once Kuei-shan said, "As long as feelings don't stick to it, then it's all right." So what kind of I, what kind of you? What kind of naming are we setting up? What kind of forming processes are we engaged in? What is true for us? If you can put a name on something, if you can generate a form around something, then you may gain a sense of managing and controlling and ordering, and feel that things are less chaotic. But there is a price to be paid for that.

Yang-shan and his friend San-sheng (Sansho; Sam Seong) once played with this business of names, using a process the Zen tradition calls play samadhi. While the word *samadhi* by itself means deep, deep meditation, or totally at one with something, play samadhi, as you might expect, is on a different level.

The best-known example of play samadhi is in the story of the hermit Jui-yen (Zuigan; Song Am), who was living all alone. Every day he would yell out to himself:

"Master!"

And then he would answer, "Yes?"

"Keep clear."

"Yes."

"Don't be deceived by others, any time, any place."

"Yes, yes."

So two minds appeared. We all do it: We talk to ourselves. Jui-yen was fortunate that he had only two minds; most of us have quite a few more than two! Jui-yen played spontaneously with this process that we all engage in.

Yang-shan and San-sheng also played with the process of naming and unnaming. But you have to understand a little something before I tell their story. The names that Zen masters were known by in China were not really their names. For example, this teacher's name was Yang-shan. But Yang-shan is really the name of a mountain in China, Mount Yang, where he taught, so he became known as the Zen master of Yang-shan. If we used that system, you might call me Fourteenth Street Zen master. But then, I also have a name that was given to me when I was made a Zen master, which is Wu Kwang. Some years earlier, before I was given the name Wu Kwang, I took the five Buddhist precepts of a layperson and was given the dharma name Won Ung. But before I was Won Ung, I was given the name Richard Shrobe. And then I also had a Hebrew name, because I was raised in a Jewish family. So there are all these names, but they all refer to the same person.

Yang-shan's first name was Hui-chi. And San-sheng was originally called Hui-jan.

Our case tells how one day Yang-shan asked San-sheng, "What is your name?" Of course, he already knew what his name was because they were close friends. But here was a challenge, because from the essential point of view, there is no name, no form, no speech, no words. So is he asking about his name, or is he asking about the person himself? We can understand this best by recognizing it as a typical bit of

Zen sword play. "What is your name?" The expected answer would be simply to hit the floor, or sit in silence, or shout, Haahh!!

San-sheng, however, took a different tack. When Yang-shan asked, "What is your name?" San-sheng answered, "Hui-chi." But Hui-chi is Yang-shan's name, not San-sheng's. Here he was essentially saying two things: First, he was telling Yang-shan, "If you're going to take away my name and make me have no name, then I'll take away your name. Give me your name." But second, he was saying that Yang-shan is San-sheng; San-sheng is Yang-shan. He was saying that all the separate names and positions we assign to ourselves are not the whole picture, because in essence I am you and you are me. We are all essentially interconnected and are supporting each other. I am Hui-chi; you are Hui-jan; I am Hui-jan; you are Hui-chi.

When Yang-shan asked, "What is your name?" and San Sheng replied, "Hui-chi," Yang-shan said, "Hui-chi? That's me." And San-sheng said, "Oh, then I'm Hui-jan." With that he returned to the normal position: You are you; I am me. Yang-shan then laughed out loud with a big belly laugh, enjoying the whole play.

If you cut away all names, all forms, and all ideas of separateness, at that moment you perceive the absolute world. In the absolute world, there is no self, no other, no inside, no outside. That is sometimes called standing alone in the vast, wide universe. In that phrase, the word *alone* is a combination of two words: *all one*. If you look at the Old English, it is like that. Standing alone does not mean an isolated state of vacancy; it means that when we recognize the absolute point of view, we are all one. Out of that recognition of our interconnectedness springs the heart of warmth and compassion and our practice of using myriad forms as a way of unfolding and awakening. This is very important.

At the conclusion of this case is a poem that refers back to the little play these two put on. One translation says:

Both grasping, both releasing—what fellows!
Riding the tiger—marvelous skill!

The laughter ends, traceless they go.
Infinite pathos, to think of them![3]

The other translation raises a question in the first line:

Both gather in, both let go—which is fundamental?[4]

In an interchange, both of these things occur; sometimes we gather in, sometimes we open up and let go. In formal meditation practice, there is a time when we sit and everything gathers in, and there is a time when we spontaneously just let go. Zen students are always wondering which one is fundamental: Should I gather in? Should I let go? If you think about all that, you are a million miles from just practicing meditation. All those processes occur over and over again spontaneously.

Here is more of the second translation:

Both gather in, both let go—which is fundamental?
To ride a tiger always requires absolute competence.
His laughter ended, I do not know where he's gone;[5]

After this expression of great joy and great play, and not being caught by name and form, where is he now? Where will we find the true Yang-shan?

The first translation says, "The laughter ends, traceless they go," while this one suggests a question: I don't know where he's gone. The translator ends with the line:

It is only fitting eternally to stir the wind of lament.[6]

The two final lines go together: "His laughter ended, I do not know where he's gone; / It is only fitting eternally to stir the wind of lament." It is an interesting poem in conjunction with the case, which is so playful, with laughter resounding in the last line. Two sentiments—one happy, the other sad, maybe wistful—are being expressed here. That apparent contradiction is very human. It is our experience of living in the world. A great piece of literature may offer something similar when you find yourself absorbed in its story. You become one with the characters as they unfold, almost as if you have found a new family or new friends. Then you come to the last chapter and the book ends. Sometimes you feel sadness and loss: It is over, and you cannot recapture the experience. Even if you read the book a second time, it would not be the same.

That mix of sadness and happiness can also appear when you listen to a piece of music. Recently I had that experience while listening to some songs of Duke Ellington. The songs had the flavor of a particular period in the history of American jazz. I sensed an exquisiteness to them, linked to that era, but at that same moment I realized that their time is no longer here. And simultaneously with the pleasure, a feeling of sadness arose. We might also have that feeling when we admire some historical figure or read a story of someone whose life inspires us, although the person may have lived hundreds of years ago.

The last lines of the verse: "His laughter ended, I do not know where he's gone; / It is only fitting eternally to stir the wind of lament" mean that if you are going to enter into laughter and joy, then there will also be this other side to it. You cannot deny one side by having the other. They are a completion, those two.

Here is one more short teaching of Yang-shan's:

> Just get the root, don't worry about the branches—
> they'll naturally be there some day. If you haven't gotten
> the root, you cannot acquire the branches even if you
> study, using your intellect and emotions. Have you not
> seen how Master Kuei-shan said, "When the mentalities
> of the ordinary mortal and the saint have ended, being
> reveals true normalcy [What is true normalcy?], where
> fact and principle are not separate; this is the buddha-
> hood of being-as-is"?[7]

I hope that in our practice we all attain true normalcy, which is not defined by ideas of any kind and is not going to be found by sticking names or labels on top of it.

Notes

1. Thomas Cleary, *The Five Houses of Zen* (Boston: Shambhala, 1997), 24.
2. Ibid.
3. Katsuki Sekida, trans., *Two Zen Classics: Mumonkan and Hekiganroku* (New York: Weatherhill, 1977), 328.
4. Thomas Cleary and J. C. Cleary, trans., *The Blue Cliff Record* (Boston: Shambhala, 1992), 383.
5. Ibid., 383–84.
6. Ibid., 384.
7. Cleary, 28.

CHAPTER 8

Tung-shan's No Cold or Hot

When you see a red flower, does it reveal the real in the apparent,
or the apparent in the real?

When could real and apparent ever be categorized?

What is the true intimacy of the real and the apparent?

Haahh!!

When you greet someone, the left and the right palms come together
in front of the heart and you bow at the waist.

This famous kong-an features Zen Master Tung-shan (Tozan; Dong
Sahn), founder of the Chinese Soto sect. It is case 43 in *The Blue Cliff
Record.*

A monk asked Tung Shan, "When cold and hot come, how can
we avoid them?"

Tung Shan said, "Why don't you go to the place where there
is no cold or hot?"

The monk said, "What is the place where there is no cold or
hot?"

Tung Shan said, "When cold, cold kills you; when hot, heat
kills you."[1]

Zen Master Seung Sahn has a short commentary on this kong-an:

> [Tung Shan's] speech is wonderful! He understands correct situation and action.
>
> Are hot and cold inside or outside? If you find the correct answer, you attain [Tung Shan's] original face.[2]

Tung-shan lived in China between 806 and 869. As a young boy, he studied the Heart Sutra with a teacher. When he got to the lines "no eyes, no ears, no nose, no tongue, no body, no mind," he touched his face and said, "Teacher, I have eyes, ears, nose, tongue, body, mind. Why does the sutra say I do not?" Taken aback, his interlocutor responded, "I'm not your teacher." Then he told Tung-shan to call on a Zen master who was a successor of the great Zen teacher Ma-tsu (Baso; Ma Jo), who had lived a few generations earlier. There had been two great teachers in China: Ma-tsu and Shih-t'ou (Sekito; Shi Hu). Each had many students, and all the main teaching lines that eventually evolved came from them.

Tung-shan followed his teacher's orders and studied with that Zen master for a while before he began traveling about. During his travels, he had contact with Zen Master Nan-ch'uan (Nansen; Nam Cheon), one of Ma-tsu's main disciples, and with Zen Master Kuei-shan (Isan; Wi Sahn), who was also in Ma-tsu's lineage. Eventually Tung-shan became a disciple of Zen Master Yun-yen (Ungan), who was of the lineage of Shih-t'ou, and received transmission from him.

If you attach to the literal meaning of this kong-an, you will get stuck, and you will not be able to perceive its true meaning and direction. Maybe it will help to look at similar language in a story about Zen Master Chao-chou (Joshu; Joju). One day Chao-chou called on a hermit and asked, "Do you have it? Do you have it?" In answer, the hermit held up one fist. Chao-chou said, "The water is too shallow to anchor here" and walked away. Later Chao-chou called on a second hermit and again asked, "Do you have it? Do you have it?" This hermit also held up one fist, but this time Chao-chou bowed and said, "You are a great person, free to give and take, free to kill and give life." In Zen Master Wu-men's (Mumon; Mu Mun) poem after this case, he says:

> Eye, a shooting star.
> Spirit, lightning.
> Death sword,
> Life sword.[3]

The poem points to the same realm as Tung-shan's kong-an: Tung-shan says, "When cold, cold kills you; when hot, heat kills you." Robert Aitken Roshi translates this line as "When it's cold you freeze to death; when it's hot you swelter to death."[4] And Suzuki Roshi might say, When it's cold, you should be cold Buddha; when it's hot, you should be hot Buddha.

Let us return to the last line of Tung-shan's emphatic teaching to the monk, "When cold, cold kills you; when hot, heat kills you." That line contains everything: You can see the absolute and the phenomenal; you can see substance and function together; you can see compassion and wisdom being expressed. You can also see that the clarity of complete action attuned to the immediate situation is the essence of both practice and realization. That is important: A complete action attuned to the immediate situation is the essence of our practice and the essence of realization. Nothing beyond that.

Aitken Roshi has a short commentary on this case. It appears in an introduction to a translation of *The Record of Tung-shan*. Aitken Roshi says, "Tung-shan Liang-chieh was intimate with the source of all categories . . . ." What is the source of all categories? That's a big question, and it points to the mind before thought. "Tung-shan Liang-chieh was intimate with the source of all categories, and thus he could present their unity and their particular virtues with vivid clarity."[5] "Their unity" is similar to the statement in the Heart Sutra, "Form is emptiness, emptiness is form." The one is the many, the many is the one, but their particular virtues are not annihilated by that; at the same time, form is just form and emptiness is just emptiness.

Aitken Roshi's statement—that Tung-shan was intimate with the source of all categories and thus could present their unity and their particular virtues with vivid clarity—refers to a teaching style that exists in the Soto school. Tung-shan had a system of teaching that was called the five ranks. Zen masters of all schools appreciate this teaching device and have used it in one form or another. It is mostly about the relationship between absolute and relative, or phenomenal and absolute, or, as I said at the beginning, the real and the apparent. Different terms are used in different versions of this teaching. Sometimes Tung-shan talked about king and minister. King represents the absolute side; minister represents the functioning-in-the-world side. Sometimes he used the terms the straight and the crooked—straight being absolute, crooked being relative. This was Tung-shan's teaching style.

Then Aitken Roshi goes further: "The reason you die with the cold is that you dwell where there is neither cold nor heat. The reason you die with the birdsong is that you dwell where there is neither sound nor silence. Dying with the cold or the birdsong is the great life of cold or the birdsong."[6] That is an important point. On the one side, we have dying—dying with the cold, dying with the birdsong. On the other side, we have the great life of cold and of the birdsong. So Wu-men says, "Death sword, / Life sword." But are those two swords or one sword? Are they separate or the same?

Tung-shan's successor Ts'ao-shan (Sozan; Cho Sahn) once asked a monk, "When it's so hot, where will you go to avoid it?" The monk said, "I'll avoid it inside a boiling cauldron, within the coals of a furnace." Ts'ao-shan then asked, "How can it be avoided in a boiling cauldron or amongst the coals of a furnace?" The monk rejoined, "The multitude of sufferings cannot reach there."

This means that essentially we live in openness and clarity from the very beginning. Moment by moment, everything emerges from this openness and returns to it. But, for some set of reasons, we begin to ignore that basic fact of our existence, and the basic fact of our connection with each and every other existence and with the vast, wide, universal existence. We begin to contract and become smaller and smaller in particular ways and define ourselves in particular ways: I'm this, but I'm not that. I'm good, but I'm not bad. I'm bad, but I'm not good. And if you then identify with that contraction and solidify it and stand your ground in the solidity of those limited definitions, then at the moment of waking up, at the moment of dropping self-contraction, you feel like you are dying, like you are losing yourself. That is the point of the statements that the great life of cold kills you and the birdsong kills you.

Two articles in *Primary Point*, the magazine of the Kwan Um School of Zen, relate to the point of Tung-shan's kong-an. One of them reports on a workshop on death, dying, and kong-ans. You could paraphrase the essence of the workshop as, If you dwell in the place of no hot and no cold, of neither sound nor silence, of just complete don't-know, then the possibilities of compassion and connection emerge. This workshop was offered by Zen Master Soeng Hyang (Barbara Rhodes), who is a hospice nurse in Rhode Island, and by Kwang Myong Sunim, who works as a pastoral counselor with terminally ill patients.

Kwang Myong Sunim reported in the workshop: "An ongoing practice for me is trying to sit with a patient who is vomiting—I still find it hard to keep my center when a patient is vomiting blood or fecal matter! There is initially a reflexive response to protect oneself—to grab a towel and duck out of the way. But if I can stay in the room and at the bedside, the purely physical revulsion and disgust passes and only then can I be of some service to that person; perhaps wiping their forehead and mouth with a slightly damp, cool cloth. In the midst of the entire stink and mess [Seen from one perspective, this might be a description of our entire life in the world, not just in the sickroom!], a deeply profound meeting transpires! It is one thing having romantic notions about helping the terminally ill, or having blissful ideas about meditation practice. However, the reality is something quite different and can be profoundly confronting if there is an 'I' who wants to help, or if this 'I' wants to attain enlightenment."[7]

This is very much to the point of Tung-shan's kong-an: "When cold, cold kills you; when hot, heat kills you." If you hold I, there is a problem.

The magazine's second article is by a Chinese nun, Zen Master Dae Kwan, who describes a situation that arose following the death of my dharma brother Zen Master Su Bong in 1994. Zen Master Su Bong was the guiding teacher of the Hong Kong Zen Center. At the age of fifty, while giving interviews one day, he had a massive heart attack and died in the interview room. Before his sudden death, he had many followers in Hong Kong, who were attracted to him for his vivid personality and his clear teaching.

"After his death," Dae Kwan Sunim reports, "half of the students left. Those who remained were very good and were very supportive. Around that time, Zen Master Seung Sahn came to Hong Kong and gave us some very good teaching. He asked me one question, 'Is the Zen Center OK?' I said, 'Bad news.'" She told him that the Zen Center might have to leave their apartment and that people were not coming to the Zen Center for practice. "At that, Zen Master Seung Sahn said, 'Don't worry about people coming or not coming. Your practice is very important.' So Zen Master Seung Sahn told us to do 1,000 bows every day and a *kido* every day."[8]

Kido is a form of meditation practice. *Ki* means "energy"—it is the same *ki* that you see in terms like *aikido*—and *do* means "path." *Kido* literally means "energy path." In the practice of kido, you chant a mantra or the name of a buddha or bodhisattva over and over again, using rhythm instruments as accompaniment. This practice can become a powerful focal point for mind energy. Zen Master Seung Sahn's point was, Don't worry whether or not people are coming or whether or not they like you. Just practice strongly every day.

Dae Kwan Sunim continues, "So I did that every day, and finally it happened. The owner said, 'You have to move!' . . . But I never questioned my teacher. I told him the bad news, 'We have to leave the apartment, and maybe we won't have a Zen Center any more.' Then Zen Master Seung Sahn said, 'No problem. You make money.'"[9]

At that, Dae Kwan Sunim said, "But I'm a nun. In the West . . . I think monks can go out to work, but in Asia they cannot."[10] In

Chinese Buddhism, monks and nuns have a special position in society. A monastic cannot just go and get a job somewhere. His or her sole job is to stay in the temple and represent the buddha dharma for everyone else.

"So I said, 'Sir, how do I make money?'"[11] And Zen Master Seung Sahn replied that they should practice kido for seven days, seven nights, nonstop, twenty-four hours a day, chanting *Hwa Om Soeng Jung*.

Hwa Om Soeng Jung is a mantra considered to have a certain kind of miraculous power. *Hwa Om* is the Korean name for the Avatamsaka Sutra. *Hwa Om Soeng Jung* refers to the assembly who were there to hear the Buddha preach this sutra. According to the legend, human beings could not hear the teaching of this sutra; only bodhisattvas and unusual beings who possess magical powers could hear. Thus, according to tradition, if you chant this mantra nonstop, you can connect with some unusual power.

Dae Kwan Sunim continues, "At that time only one student was there, but we did the kido anyway. And guess what? Many people came to our kido! Some of them came just to do the kido. They didn't even know us; they just came. Zen Master Seung Sahn said, 'If you do this kido, some miracle will appear.' I never believed in miracles, but I believe in practice."[12]

That last sentence is important: "I never believed in miracles, but I believe in practice." Miracles are not important, but practicing over and over and over again, making practice one's life, that itself is already a miracle. Dae Kwan Sunim goes on to say, "So I only practiced. Miracle? I didn't even want to think about it."[13]

Zen Master Dae Kwan has been a serious practitioner for a long time. She went to Thailand and practiced Theravadin Buddhism, living alone in a cave for two years. She continued her studies in Thailand with a teacher for ten years, until she met Zen Master Seung Sahn. She believes in practice; hers has been a life of practice.

"When we began those seven days, we had nothing," Dae Kwan Sunim says. "Our bank account was less than 100,000 Hong Kong dollars. If you wanted to buy an apartment, it cost more than three million dollars. We did the kido, and it was very interesting. Many people gave us donations! Many people helped us. . . . On the fifth day, we were able to find an apartment. On the seventh day, we were able to borrow the money from the bank, and . . . buy the apartment."[14]

This relates to Tung-shan's "When cold, cold kills you; when hot, heat kills you." Dae Kwan Sunim says, "What I'm trying to share is how our teaching connects with our everyday life, especially when you are really facing something [difficult,] . . . . especially when you have nowhere to go, [and] you have no choice."[15] That is another important point in practice: nowhere to go and no choice. Usually we think we have many places to go and many, many choices in our lives. But in fact, from the most fundamental standpoint, we have nowhere else to go, and we have only one choice.

If you think your life is any different from that, you are mistaken. When you really face the fact that there is nowhere to go and no choice, then you enter your situation completely. Your mind does not keep saying, Well, maybe I'll do this, maybe I'll do that. There is no choice. There is only this moment, moment by moment by moment. And at that point, you can open to the simplicity of your being and of your connection with others. From that, clear action is possible, compassionate meeting is possible.

Cold kills you, hot kills you, nowhere to go, and no choice.

A student asked me recently, "Is the purpose of enlightenment to avoid strong emotions?" My answer is that to have strong emotions is one thing; to be swayed by them is a different thing; the search for enlightenment is a third thing. And *that* is a big problem. If you are approaching practice with the attitude of suppressing emotions, you will give yourself a big headache and will get further and further from actualizing and being who and what you are.

The faith of the Zen tradition is that you are already buddha from the beginning. Not that you will become buddha, but that you are already awakened, that you already possess enlightened nature. At any particular moment, true nature and your moment-to-moment existence are intimately identified with one another. At any particular moment, if you stop searching for something out in front of you and just come back to yourself—What am I?—at that moment you are just you. If you attain this not-knowing mind, then there is no grasping. Then, if enlightenment comes, wonderful. If enlightenment goes, that's also wonderful. That attitude itself *is* enlightenment. Not making anything, not holding anything, not getting stuck with anything. Our practice is to manifest that spirit over and over.

If you look at what we do in formal Zen meditation, for example—besides the fact that we sit in a particular way and become still—we essentially don't try to get rid of any thought or any feeling. Likewise, we don't cling to any particular thought or state of mind or any particular feeling. We let everything come and go freely. Just perceive, moment by moment. That practice is a cultivation of nongrasping. That nongrasping is the essence of your true being. If you sit with that attitude, if sadness appears, at that moment you're just sad. If happiness appears, at that moment you're just happy. If pain appears, at that moment there's just pain. You could say sadness kills you at that moment, happiness kills you at that moment, pain in your legs kills you at that moment, the sound of the siren from the fire engine down the street kills you at that moment. But that killing is a coming to life. You connect with what is.

So there is a difference between being pulled by emotion and having emotion. We are all human beings, so we naturally have thoughts, we naturally have emotions, we naturally have sensations, we naturally have a body, we naturally have relationships. They're all just aspects of our natural being. But if you begin to get stuck in particular ways, then your emotions pull you around by the nose. Then you are caught.

There is a famous story about Zen Master Kyong Ho Sunim, who lived in Korea from 1849 to 1912. Originally he was a scholar-monk, but at a certain point he realized that all his scholarship did not satisfy his primary desire to know who and what he was. He gave up teaching the sutras and lived in a small hermitage, just practicing sitting meditation. Then one day a layman, Mr. Lee, asked Kyong Ho's attendant, "What is Kyong Ho Sunim doing these days? I heard he dismissed all his students." The attendant replied, "These days my teacher is practicing very hard. He only sits, eats, and lies down." Mr. Lee said, "If your teacher Kyong Ho Sunim only sits, eats, and lies down, he'll be reborn as a cow." At that the student got quite angry and said, "My teacher is one of the greatest monks in all of Korea. How can you say he'll be reborn as a cow?" Mr. Lee said, "No, no, that's not the way to answer me."

Mr. Lee is one of those enigmatic figures who appear in Zen stories. Sometimes it's an old man, or an old woman running a teahouse, or some layman, someone who doesn't appear to be an official Zen teacher.

Then the student asked, "Well, how should I have answered you?" Mr. Lee replied, "If Kyong Ho Sunim is reborn as a cow, it will be as a cow with no nostrils." Then the attendant was even more confused. "A cow with no nostrils, what does that mean?" Mr. Lee said, "Go back to the temple and ask Kyong Ho Sunim." The attendant went back, knocked on the hermitage door, and when Kyong Ho Sunim opened it the attendant said, "I ran into your friend Mr. Lee." "Oh, what did Mr. Lee have to say?" "He said you'll be reborn as a cow if you only eat, sit, and lie down. Then I got angry with him," and he told the rest of the story. When he got to the line "If Kyong Ho Sunim is reborn as a cow, it will be a cow with no nostrils," Kyong Ho Sunim's eyes suddenly brightened, his whole face became luminous, and he stood up and walked out of the room, ending his retreat. Then he wrote his enlightenment poem, with these first two lines:

> When I heard about the cow with no nostrils
> the whole world became my home.

It is still common in Asia to see an ox being used to till the fields and work the rice paddies. He can be directed by pulling on the reins that are attached to his nostrils. If, however, you are an ox with no nostrils, that means you cannot be pulled this way or that way. If you are being pulled by your emotions, then your emotions use you. But if you cut off your attachment to thinking, then emotions are just emotions. They find their appropriate place in your being, and they become the energy that fuels certain kinds of interactions. If you have no feeling or passion, how are you going to have compassion? If you don't understand what sorrow is, how can you help another person who is in sorrow? If you don't know what joy is, how can you be happy for someone doing well? Nothing needs to be discarded; each thing just needs to find its appropriate place. First course: Don't seek after enlightenment; only come back to your original home. Then everything, little by little, will become clear.

Notes

1. Seung Sahn, trans., *The Blue Cliff Record* (Cumberland, RI: Kwan Um School of Zen, 1983), 36.
2. Seung Sahn, *The Whole World Is a Single Flower* (Rutland, VT: Tuttle, 1992), 210.
3. Seung Sahn, trans., *The Mu Mun Kwan* (Cumberland, RI: Kwan Um School of Zen, 1983), 13.
4. William F. Powell, trans., *The Record of Tung-shan* (Honolulu: University of Hawaii Press, 1986), vii.
5. Ibid.
6. Ibid.
7. *Primary Point* 18, no. 1 (2000): 12.
8. Ibid., 14–15.
9. Ibid., 15.
10. Ibid.
11. Ibid.
12. Ibid.
13. Ibid.
14. Ibid.
15. Ibid.

CHAPTER 9

Te-shan Carrying His Bowls

Does hitting the floor with the Zen master's stick reveal the first word?
If you say that it does, then rock and bamboo also reveal the first word.

Does hitting the floor with the Zen master's stick reveal the last word?
If you say it does, then you understand one but have not yet grasped two.
Be careful, or you will get caught in the cave of emptiness.

The first word and the last word, are these one or two? If you say one,
you have missed it by a mile. If you say two, the Zen stick will hit you.

What can you do?

Haahh!!

My job is writing this. Just now, your job is reading.

This is a well-known kong-an connected with the phrase "the last word." It is case 13 in the collection called *Wu-men-kuan* (*Mumonkan; Mu Mun Kwan*), and it also appears in *Book of Serenity*.

One day Te-shan came into the dharma room carrying his bowls. The house master, Hsueh-feng, said, "Old Master, the bell has not yet been rung and the drum has not yet been struck. Where are you going, carrying your bowls?" Te-shan returned to the Master's room. Hsueh-feng told the head monk, Yen-t'ou.

Yen-t'ou said, "Great master Te-shan does not understand the last word."

Te-shan heard this and sent for Yen-t'ou. "Do you not approve of me?" he demanded. Then Yen-t'ou whispered in the master's ear. Te-shan was relieved.

Next day, on the rostrum, making his dharma speech, Te-shan was really different than before. Yen-t'ou went to the front of the dharma room, laughed loudly, clapped his hands and said, "Great joy! The old master has understood the last word! From now on, no one can check him."[1]

After the case, Zen Master Wu-men (Mumon; Mu Mun) has a short poem:

> Understand first word,
> Then understand last word.
> Last word and first word
> Are not one word.[2]

Wu-men also has a commentary after the case. In his usual style, the commentary appears to be critical and caustic. But if you understand the style of Chinese humor he is using, it is actually a compliment. Wu-men says:

> As for the last word, neither Yen-t'ou nor Te-shan have ever heard it, even in a dream. When I examine this point, I find they are like puppets on a shelf.[3]

Some people say the phrase "they are like puppets on a shelf" means that the two of them put on a big show for everybody. But I think what he actually means here is that the puppet is something that is neither vital nor alive in itself; it is animated by someone pulling a string or sticking a hand in it. On first glance, you may think Wu-men is saying Yen-t'ou and Te-shan are not alive, vital, or free; they are like puppets.

But as always, his humor is backwards. He is actually affirming their action as vital, alive, and to the point.

Zen Master Seung Sahn, who also includes this story in his book of kong-ans *The Whole World Is a Single Flower*, makes a comment that is even more terse: "Three dogs chase each other's tails in a circle, following the smell, looking for food."[4]

Before going on, let us take a look at the protagonists. Te-shan (Tokusan; Duk Sahn) was a famous Zen master who lived in China from the late seven hundreds to the middle eight hundreds. We already met him in chapter 6, "Te-shan Carrying His Bundle." At the time of this story, he is an old man in his early eighties. He passed away a few years later. Te-shan was famous for the use of his stick; he was known for saying, "I give you thirty blows with my stick!" One day Te-shan came to the dharma room and said, "If you open your mouth, thirty blows. If you keep your mouth closed, still you get thirty blows." Not surprisingly, Te-shan became known all over China as the Zen master of the thirty blows.

Yen-t'ou (Ganto; Am Du), the head monk in the story, and Hsueh-feng (Seppo; Seol Bong), the head of the kitchen (the rice cook or housemaster) were considerably younger than Te-shan. At the time of this story, Yen-t'ou was about thirty-five years old, and Hseuh-feng was about forty-five. They had known each other for quite a while and were close friends. They had already been monks for fifteen or twenty years, had traveled around to most of the major Zen temples in China, and had spent time with various Zen masters. By the time of this story, Yen-t'ou was confident of his experience and attainment and did not defer to anyone. Hsueh-feng, although he had had a number of experiences along the way, was not yet secure and confident of himself. But both held responsible positions in this monastery. If the Zen master is the captain, the head monk is the first lieutenant, who always presides over the meditation hall. The kitchen master must prepare meals that respond to everybody's needs. In the traditional Buddhist monastery, food is viewed as medicine, and the kitchen master's job is seen as service to the community as well as an opportunity to practice meditation in action.

Before we go into the case, be aware that certain kong-ans may be interpreted in several different ways. Teachers and teaching lineages may make different points using the same kong-an, to emphasize particular aspects of practice or realization. That does not mean one teacher is correct and another is not; it does mean that embellishment may be heaped on to make a teaching point.

The main core of Zen teaching, however, is the bare bones of what is there. In a certain sense then, embellishing a story takes away from the central teaching: Don't embellish anything, just be with it as it is.

This story, of course, is open to a lot of embellishment and a lot of different views, because its language is vague. First, look at the phrase "the last word." What is the last word of Zen? Next, the incident where the head monk whispers something in the master's ear, and the master is relieved. What was it that he whispered? Then, when the Zen master mounts the rostrum the next day, he gives a dharma talk considerably different than usual. It does not say what kind of dharma speech he gives, just that it was different. This allows a wide array of speculation.

Let's go back and look at the story. The first paragraph says that Zen Master Te-shan came into the dharma room carrying his bowls. Then the housemaster said, "Old Master, the bell has not been rung, and the drum has not been struck. Where are you going, carrying your bowls?" He was basically saying, Why are you here? You're in the wrong place at the wrong time. At that, Te-shan, without saying anything, turned around and returned to his room.

This seems a little strange. The Zen master has made a mistake. He is in the wrong place at the wrong time. Some people conclude that returning to his room in silence is his way of teaching something. Others, however, say that is his second mistake: First, he is in the wrong place at the wrong time; then he does not handle the situation well: two strikes.

At the end of the *Wu-men-kuan,* Zen Master Wu-men offers some cautions. One says: "To be alert and never unclear is to wear chains and an iron yoke."[5]

That sounds rather curious. Usually we think of the formalities of

Zen practice—sitting, chanting, and walking meditation—as exercises in being alert and becoming clear. But here it says that to be alert and never unclear is to bind yourself with chains and an iron yoke. The meaning is that even alertness and clarity, if they become a pursuit—something you aim at for gaining a sense of mastery—will turn into bindings and traps.

Someone told me a story about Zen Master Seung Sahn that may help explain this idea. Once he was at the Dharma Zen Center in Los Angeles and was supposed to go up to the Empty Gate Zen Center in Berkeley. But at the airport he somehow got on the wrong plane and wound up in Albuquerque. With a lot of finessing, he was rerouted to Berkeley. When he finally got off the plane there, he said to the person who met him, "Today was stupid practicing day." Sometimes practice is stupid practicing day, sometimes alert practicing day; sometimes practice is clear practicing day, sometimes unclear practicing day. But every day is practicing day.

In the kong-an, Te-shan is in a similar position to Seung Sahn's position that day, not particularly clear and sharp. But it does not seem to be bothering him much. After all, he is already eighty years old. Then Hsueh-feng, the kitchen master, tells Yen-t'ou, the head monk, about the Zen master's curious behavior: The Zen master came down at the wrong time, carrying his bowls, and then just turned around and returned to his room without saying anything. Yen-t'ou's response could be rephrased to say, Great though he is, old Te-shan still doesn't understand the last word. This phrase, "the last word," is the core of the kong-an. It was a teaching phrase Yen-t'ou used many times throughout his life. But what is the last word? What does it mean?

The first meaning is that Te-shan is not following his situation. He is in the wrong place at the wrong time, and because he does not follow his situation, his functioning is not clear. In that sense, the last word means to function clearly according to the situation and according to the particular relationship of the moment. Looked at a little more broadly, however, we may see another meaning: The last word of Zen is not some final attainment, some absolute end point. Instead, the last word of Zen refers to the ongoing practice of moment Zen—activity that is not being colored by ideas of the past or memory that is leaking into the present moment. If you practice and attain moment Zen, then you perceive clearly the situation of this very moment, your correct relationship to this situation, and the correct functioning that spontaneously emerges out of that perception of the situation and relationship. The last word is primarily about action.

If you are going to practice the moment Zen of the last word, you have to be clear about your condition, so you can enter into the situation and join with the relationship of the moment. Essentially the last word means you and the world are not two. The world is in you, and you are in the world. That means cut off the idea of duality.

Philosophical Buddhism has a teaching scheme called the four wisdoms. These represent different aspects of practice and of clear mind. The first wisdom is called universal nature wisdom. If you attain the mind before thinking, you attain universal nature wisdom.

The second wisdom is called great mirror wisdom, meaning that if your mind is empty, then it clearly reflects the whole panorama of your experience. Thus great mirror wisdom means completely empty, completely full: completely empty of any idea or conception, especially of a substantial, separate, self-sufficient self; completely empty of any idea of self-sufficiency; and completely full of your connection with the many possibilities of this universe.

The third is called observing wisdom, meaning that you begin to discern the distinctness and specificity of each and every thing, rather than just perceiving a panorama. At that point, you perceive that black is black, and white is white, that sky is high, and ground is wide.

The last one is called perfecting of action wisdom. Here, if you attain the previous three, you can begin to perfect action and commit to helping others.

In the Zen Buddhist tradition, there are many concrete images that represent this last word, or perfecting of action wisdom. Among them is a series of ten pictures called the ox-herding pictures. The ox represents mind.

The first picture, "Seeing the Footprints of the Ox," represents the moment when you catch a glimpse of what original mind is like. Others are titled "Finding the Ox" and "Reining In the Ox." Then there is a picture of "Riding the Ox," which has a little person sitting on top of the ox. After that is "Leading the Ox Back Home." Further along is one called "Both Ox and Person Forgotten," which is just an empty circle. The very last picture in the series shows a chubby little guy with a round belly and a wine gourd slung across his chest. His hands are open in a gesture of giving and receiving. This picture is titled "Entering the Marketplace with Helping Hands." Chogyam Trungpa Rinpoche, the great Tibetan teacher, commenting on this last picture in the series says, "You destroy whatever needs to be destroyed, you subdue what needs to be subdued, and you care for whatever needs your care."[6] That is perfecting of action wisdom, the expression of wisdom and compassion completely interfused.

The spirit of universal compassion is sometimes represented as a female form with a thousand hands surrounding her in a big circle. In each hand is an eye. This is called the Thousand Hands and Eyes Bodhisattva of Compassion. Once, two monks were discussing this image. One said to the other, "What does the Bodhisattva of Compassion do with so many hands and eyes?" The other monk replied, "It's something like, in the middle of the night, reaching back and straightening your pillow." When you are asleep in the middle of the night and your pillow is out of place, you do not think about it, you just spontaneously reach back and adjust it. At that point, the other monk said, "Oh, now I understand." The first monk then asked, "Well, what is it that you understand?" The other monk replied, "All over the body are hands and eyes." The first monk said, "You've said a lot there, but you've only said eighty percent." "Oh, and how would you say it, brother?" demanded the other. "Throughout the body are hands and eyes," answered the first monk.

"Throughout the body are hands and eyes" represents the complete embodiment of compassion and skillful activity. *Eyes* means clear seeing of the current situation and relationship. *Hands* means doing something governed by the wisdom of your perception. "Throughout the body are hands and eyes" means completely manifesting the one with that spirit of compassionate activity in the world. In one sense, you could say that each of us is one of these hands and eyes. But at the same time, we are also the complete totality of all the hands and eyes. That is the essence of what the phrase "the last word" points to.

Let's continue with the kong-an. After the head monk, Yen-t'ou, has made his pronouncement that the old master does not understand the last word, Zen Master Te-shan sends for him. He has heard about this comment. Probably everybody in the monastery is now buzzing that the head monk said the Zen master doesn't understand the last word. But when Yen-t'ou comes to his room and whispers something in the master's ear, Te-shan is relieved.

Some people say that Yen-t'ou tells the Zen master not to worry—that his true intention in saying that Te-shan didn't know the last word was simply to get Hsueh-feng's attention. Now the Zen master and head monk can collude in some skillful fashion to help Hsueh-feng have an awakening. And maybe in fact that is what happened. It is a nice idea, one brother looking out for the other, an act of compassion. But you have to torture the text a little to arrive at that meaning. The bare bones of the story are just the head monk's statement. Many people might think that the head monk in a monastery would never say something like that about the Zen master, especially because this takes place in China, with all its formalities and hierarchical social protocols, like respect for the teacher and respect for your parents.

But the story says that the head monk did make the statement, the Zen master did get upset and did send for him, demanding, "Don't you approve of me?" And at that point there is a problem between them. Now the question becomes, how do you repair a strained relationship? We all have found ourselves in situations like that. It is important that the head monk and Zen master see things in accordance with one another, just like husband and wife, boyfriend and girlfriend, two close friends, or two coworkers. How do you reestablish the harmony of your relationship? If you want someone to listen to something you have to say, what can you do in that situation to get them to listen? Reestablishing harmony and rapport is essential for all beings.

Other stories about Yen-t'ou offer a flavor of his style and temperament and help us see whether he was capable of blatantly saying, The old boy doesn't understand the last word. Especially pertinent are some of Yen-t'ou's interchanges with teachers when he was in his early to mid thirties and was traveling to various monasteries. One tells of the first time he called on Zen Master Yang-shan (Kyozan; An Sahn). As soon as he entered the dharma hall, Yen-t'ou held up his sitting mat and yelled out "Master!" Yang-shan immediately reached down and held up his whisk. (At that time, Zen masters had emblematic horsehair whisks.) When Yang-shan held up his whisk, it was as if he had said, Well, here is the sign of the Zen master. Yen-t'ou said, "An undeniable expert," turned and left.

Then, when Yen-t'ou first came to call on Te-shan, he entered the dharma room and stood in front of Te-shan, holding up his mat and looking up at Te-shan, who was sitting on the high seat. Te-shan said, "Well?" At that, Yen-t'ou just snorted, "Bah!" Te-shan then said, "Where is my fault?" To which Yen-t'ou replied, "A second offense is not permitted," turned around, and left the room. The next day he came again. This time he stood next to Te-shan, who said, "Aren't you that fellow who just arrived yesterday?" Yen-t'ou replied, "Yes, sir." Te-shan said, "Where did you learn that empty-headedness?" Now that sounds like an insult, but in fact it is a remark of recognition. If you are going to function clearly and perceive clearly, you have to have emptied out all of the stuff in your head. Yen-t'ou replied, "I never deceive myself." Then Te-shan said, "In the future you shouldn't turn your back on me." Some translations say that Te-shan said, "Some time in the future you will shit on my head."

It is an interesting interchange when Te-shan asks, "Where did you learn that empty-headedness?" and Yen-t'ou just says, "I never deceive myself." Most of us are repeatedly deceiving ourselves. All around us we may see people dying, yet we think that somehow we are going to live forever. There is always tomorrow to get something done. When the alarm clock rings in the morning, telling us to get up and sit meditation, we turn on the snooze alarm and doze for another fifteen minutes. We also repeatedly deceive ourselves with ideas like,

I'm not worthy, I'm not deserving, I'm not very good. Usually we don't consider such thoughts as deception. More often we think of self-deception as inflating ourselves, thinking of ourselves as better, more talented than we actually are. But the fact is, the more primary deception is that we make ourselves feel, over and over, less than we actually are.

Recently someone told me a story. She said, "From childhood on, I always thought that I was stupid. Then I got married, had a couple of children, and I still thought I was stupid. Then I went back to college and did very well, but I still thought I was stupid—that somehow I must have been fooling the instructors, and that sooner or later I was going to take one course where they would see through me and see just how stupid I was." Many of us harbor a view like that, however subtle, but it goes on and on and on.

But when Yen-t'ou said, "I never deceive myself," he meant, "I don't get caught up in any ideas of better or worse, deserving or undeserving, good or bad. I never deceive myself with these thoughts about image. I just clearly perceive the essential."

On another occasion, Yen-t'ou came to Te-shan's room. Standing at the threshold, he asked, "Is it holy or is it ordinary?" Immediately Te-shan shouted, "Katz!" Yen-t'ou bowed to him. Later, when Zen Master Tung-shan (Tozan; Dong Sahn) heard about this interchange, he said, "Anybody but Yen-t'ou would have found it difficult to respond." When Yen-t'ou heard about Tung-shan's comment, he said, "The old master of Tung-shan doesn't understand good from bad. He didn't understand that at that time I was holding up the old boy with one hand and putting him down with the other."

In another story about Yen-t'ou, the housemaster Hsueh-feng asked Te-shan, "What doctrine is used to teach people in our sect?" Te-shan answered, "Our sect has no words. In reality there is no doctrine that can be given to people." When Yen-t'ou heard of this, he said, "The old man Te-shan has a spine as strong as iron. It can't be broken. Even so, when it comes to the way of expounding the teaching, he still lacks something." This was Yen-t'ou's style. He did not hesitate to open his mouth and speak his mind.

Now we come to the last part of the kong-an, when Yen-t'ou whispered whatever it was that he whispered in the master's ear and Te-shan was relieved. The next day, the story says, when Te-shan mounted the rostrum, his dharma speech was different than before. Yen-t'ou applauded and said, "Great joy!"—the old boy had finally got hold of the last word. "From now on, no one can check him." One question is, if his dharma speech was different than before, what kind did he usually give? Zen Master Yuan-Wu (Engo), the compiler of *The Blue Cliff Record*, once said that Te-shan "could scold the Buddhas and revile the Patriarchs, pummel the wind and beat the rain."[7] One of Te-shan's more typical dharma speeches reads:

> I see differently from our ancestors. Here there is neither
> patriarch nor Buddha. Bodhidharma is an old stinking
> barbarian. Shakyamuni is a dry toilet strip. Manjushri
> and Samantabhadra are dung-heap coolies. *Samyak-
> sambodhi* and subtle perception are nothing but ordinary
> human nature freed of fetters. Bodhi and nirvana are but
> dead stumps to tie the donkeys to. The twelve divisions
> of the scriptures are only registers of ghosts, sheets
> of paper fit only for wiping the pus from your ulcers
> and tumors. All the "four fruitions" and "ten stages" are
> nothing but demons lingering in their decayed graves,
> who cannot even save themselves.[8]

This was Te-shan's usual style: "If you speak correctly, you get thirty blows. If you speak incorrectly, you also get thirty blows." When Zen Master Lin-chi (Rinzai) heard of this, he said to one of his monks, "Go there and ask him why the one who speaks correctly should get thirty blows. As soon as he begins to hit you, grab hold of his stick, push it against him, and see what he'll do." The monk did as Lin-chi had told him. Just as Te-shan went to hit him, the monk grabbed the stick and pushed it against Te-shan, who stood up and silently returned to his room. When the monk came back and told of the incident, Lin-chi said, "I always had my doubts about that old fellow. But putting that aside for a moment, did you see the real Te-shan?" As the monk fumbled for something to say, Lin-chi hit him.

Te-shan gave a speech that was different than usual, so his flexibility obviously was great, and he understood how to rise to the occasion quickly. There is one more point here. The beginning of the case says that the housemaster asked Te-shan, "Old Master, the bell has not yet been rung and the drum has not yet been struck. Where are you going carrying your bowls?" Te-shan silently returned to the master's room. Some people say that Te-shan was teaching through his silence, that he was teaching something like, Coming, going, mistake, no mistake, these are all of one seamless fabric. But even if this were so, the housemaster did not get it. Then all the complication and confusion emerged in the monastery.

The final question is, if you were Te-shan, what could you have said to the housemaster at that moment? How could you have used your mistake to give him some simple, clear Zen teaching? This is an important point. How can we use our mistakes rather than getting hung up on them? How can we be flexible and yielding, yet stand firm when it is necessary to stand firm? And how can we connect with the situation at hand and help this world in a thousand different ways, as the bodhisattva who has a thousand hands?

Notes

1. See Seung Sahn, trans., *The Mu Mun Kwan* (Cumberland, RI: Kwan Um School of Zen, 1983), 15.
2. Ibid., 16.
3. See Koun Yamada, trans., *The Gateless Gate* (Boston: Wisdom, 2004), 66.
4. Seung Sahn, *The Whole World Is a Single Flower* (Rutland, VT: Tuttle, 1992), 182.
5. Robert Aitken, trans., *The Gateless Barrier* (San Francisco: North Point Press, 1991), 289.
6. Chogyam Trungpa, *Mudra* (Berkeley: Shambhala, 1972), 92.
7. Thomas Cleary and J. C. Cleary, trans., *The Blue Cliff Record* (Boston: Shambhala, 1992), 27.
8. John C. H. Wu, *The Golden Age of Zen* (New York: Doubleday, 1996), 115.

CHAPTER 10

San-sheng's Golden Fish
Who Has Passed Through the Net

Cause is effect; effect is cause. The name for that is karma.

No cause, no effect. The name for that is true emptiness.

Cause and effect are both perfectly clear. The name for
that is great round mirror shining brightly.

But if we put aside all these designations, then what
is the living fact being pointed to?

Haahh!!

Today a cow is eating grass; tomorrow cow dung
will make good fertilizer.

San-sheng (Sansho; Sam Seong) was a successor of Zen Master
Lin-chi (Rinzai), one of the greatest Zen masters of China's T'ang
Dynasty. He was also one of just two characters in *The Blue Cliff Record*
case 49.

San-sheng asked Hsueh-feng , "I wonder, what does the
golden fish who has passed through the net use for food?"
    Hsueh-feng said, "When you come out of the net, I'll
tell you."

San-sheng said, "The teacher of fifteen hundred people, and you do not understand the point of a question."

Hsueh-feng said, "This old monk is busy taking care of the temple."[1]

After Lin-chi's death, San-sheng compiled a short book, *The Record of Lin-chi,* for which he is justly remembered today. But a frequently told story says that when Lin-chi was an old man close to dying he said to the assembly, "When I am gone, don't let the true treasure of my correct understanding of the dharma disappear from this world." At that San-sheng stepped forward and said, "Master, how could you think that we would ever let the treasure of your true understanding of the dharma disappear from this world?" Lin-chi then asked him, "If someone in the future should ask you, what would you say?" San-sheng yelled, "Katz!" This shout was an often-used device in the Lin-chi school. At that, Lin-chi looked up and said, "Who would have thought that the treasury of my correct understanding of the dharma would be entrusted to this blind donkey?" Shortly thereafter, he passed away.

The other character in case 49 is Hsueh-feng (Seppo; Seol Bong), whom we encountered in chapter 9. If I had to pick a hero from among any of the old Zen masters from China's T'ang Dynasty period, it would be Hsueh-feng. Perhaps he was not as brilliant or quick-witted as certain others, but he practiced hard and diligently over many years. He was a great example of Bodhidharma's maxim: Fall down seven, get up eight. Or, as Zen Master Seung Sahn called it, try mind.

Seung Sahn gave some of his students a lesson on try mind once when the Chogye International Zen Center of New York was young. During those years, the center moved locations several times. At first we had a residential Zen Center. This meant that early-morning practice was well attended. But when we moved, our next center was nonresidential. This meant that students had to volunteer to cover early-morning practice at 5:15 A.M. Frequently you led practice with a congregation of one—yourself. So we decided that doing away with early-morning practice would make things a lot easier for everybody.

When Zen Master Seung Sahn came on a visit to the New York center, we said to him, "Soen Sa Nim, we would like to do away with morning practice because no one is coming, and it is difficult." But he had a different idea. "If one person is strong," he said, "ten thousand people are strong"—if one person was there practicing in the morning, that place was going to become a strong spot of practice, regardless of how many others came along. What was most important was to have a consistent, ongoing daily practice.

He said, "Yes, you could do away with morning practice, but then you would not be a Zen Center any more. Maybe a Zen Club." He said it with just the right subtlety of disdain, so we knew what he was saying. Then he added, "Yes, maybe you'll be a Zen Club, and maybe sometimes I will come here and lead a retreat." Then he paused. We all looked at each other. What were we going to do? Finally we came to a silent agreement; we would continue the morning practice. We said, "Yes, we'll keep trying." He replied, "Yes, you do that. Try, try, try for ten thousand years nonstop."

That was the first time I heard that sentence, which became one of his trademark teaching phrases. "Try for ten thousand years" means to make a sincere effort moment by moment by moment. When you are doing something, just completely do it. Don't think about good, don't think about bad, don't check anything. Just become completely one with your activity. That is try mind.

Hsueh-feng understood that kind of mind or practice. It is said that wherever he went in his travels—and he traveled quite a bit, going from one assembly to another and calling on different enlightened masters—he would always carry a ladle and bucket. Then, when he got to the temple, he would volunteer to be the rice cook, not a job that most people in a Zen temple wanted. He considered that part of his diligent practice effort. He seems to have practiced hard and long with Zen Master T'ou-tzu (Tosu; Tu Ja) three different times; on nine occasions he climbed Mount Tung to practice hard and long with Zen

Master Tung-shan (Tozan; Dong Sahn). That does not mean that he went there just for a day and then left, traveling on to other places in some kind of casual manner. It means he returned nine times to the same teacher and practiced and practiced, and he went three times to another.

When Hsueh-feng was only nine years old, he asked his father if he could become a monk. His father refused. But when he was twelve, he and his father went to visit a temple where the abbot was a well-known precepts master. When the boy saw him, he said to his father, "This monk is my teacher." This time his father relented and let him stay at the monastery. At age seventeen, Hsueh-feng had his head shaved.

At age twenty-four, Hsueh-feng met a great Zen master, Ling-hsun, who was a second-generation successor in the line of Ma-ku (Mayoku; Ma Gok). Hsueh-feng stayed with this master for six years, until the master died, and then he remained in the temple another two years, observing a mourning period.

After that he started traveling, calling on different assemblies. By then he was thirty-two years old. In his travels he met his dharma brother, Yen-t'ou (Ganto; Am Du) and another monk, Chin-shan (Kinzan). The three of them traveled around together, calling on many assemblies and masters. Once Chin-shan stopped to wash his feet in a stream and saw some vegetable leaves floating in the water. This made him very happy, and he said to Hsueh-feng, "There must be a man of the Way (a hermit Zen teacher who has practiced for a long time) living on this mountain. Why don't we follow the stream and call on him?" Hsueh-feng replied, "Your wisdom eye is cloudy. If you continue to be this way, how will you help others in the future? If that monk's regard for material blessings is so careless, how could he truly be a man of the Way?" This conversation lets us know that care and carelessness are very much at the heart of this kong-an.

Later, when Hsueh-feng was serving as the rice steward in Tung-shan's monastery, Tung-shan asked him, "What are you doing?" Hsueh-feng replied, "I am cleaning the rice." Tung-shan then asked, "Are you washing the grit to get rid of the rice or washing the rice to get rid of the grit?" Hsueh-feng answered, "Both grit and rice are removed at the same time." Tung-shan said, "If that's the case, what will the assembly eat?" At that Hsueh-feng abruptly turned over the bucket, and Tung-shan said, "Your affinity is not with me; your affinity is with Zen Master Te-shan (Tokusan; Duk Sahn). You should go and call on him."

When Hsueh-feng reached Te-shan's temple, he said to the Zen master, "Does this monk share a portion of the realization of the ancients or not?" Te-shan immediately hit him and demanded, "What are you saying?" At that moment, Hsueh-feng had an awakening of some kind. By then he was about forty years old. He stayed at Te-shan's temple for another four or five years. Te-shan at that time was eighty years old.

After Te-shan died, Hsueh-feng set off again with his dharma brother, Yen-t'ou. Once they were snowed in at a place called Tortoise Mountain. While they were stranded there, Hsueh-feng spent his time practicing sitting meditation, but Yen-t'ou just slept. Hsueh-feng kept bothering Yen-t'ou by saying, "Brother, get up and practice." Yen-t'ou would reply, "Why should I?" Hsueh-feng bemoaned his fate, "Why do I have such a poor sangha brother here? Who could get any encouragement to practice from him?" Yen-t'ou chided him by saying, "You look like a clay Buddha statue in a small shrine somewhere." Hsueh-feng replied, "I can't deceive myself. My inner being is not completely at rest." Even though he had had an awakening under Te-shan, he still had some lingering doubt. Yen-t'ou said, "Oh, I am surprised to hear that. Tell me about your practice." Hsueh-feng told him the story of his first meeting with Te-shan and said, "When Te-shan hit me with a stick, it felt like the bottom of a black-lacquered bucket had dropped out." At that, Yen-t'ou shouted at him, "Don't you know that what comes in through the gate is not the true family treasure?" In other words, when someone else provokes an experience in you, that is not the true family treasure; you are still relying on something from outside. "Instead, you should let the experience come from within yourself and merge with heaven and earth." When Hsueh-feng heard that, he had a big awakening.

Later the two of them parted company. Hsueh-feng gradually established his own community and eventually had fifteen hundred students. Of those students, perhaps sixty or more became teachers in their own right. Two main schools of Zen—the Fa-yen (Hogen; Poep An) and the Yun-men (Ummon; Un Mun)—came from his line.

This case probably takes place following the death of Lin-chi in 866 or 867, when San-sheng had left Lin-chi's monastery to travel around. That would mean Hsueh-feng and San-sheng were already Zen masters, and San-sheng was most likely a guest at Hsueh-feng's monastery. This is when he turned to Hsueh-feng and said, "I wonder, what does the golden fish who has passed through the net use for food?"

Golden fish stands for the original true self. It is interesting that he does not say, I wonder what the golden fish who has jumped out of the net uses for food? Instead, he says, "the golden fish who has passed through the net." Net here means mind, thinking, complications, conceptions, all the hindrances and limitations that we put in our way by constructing a universe of our own making rather than seeing the true, simple fact of what is just in front of us.

Thus to pass through the net, from the standpoint of Zen meditation, means that practice is not primarily aimed at trying to get rid of thoughts and jump out of a net—to get free by avoiding something. Rather, it means that when you perceive clearly the nature of what your thoughts are constructed of, their transparency, their nonsubstantiality, then you pass through without eliminating anything.

This image is also interesting in another way. When you realize that the spaces in the net are very small and the golden fish is quite large, another question appears: How is it that the golden fish can pass through such a small space? When we are attached to all the notions we are making, it feels as if we do not have much space. Breathing may even become difficult at that time. But when you see clearly the nature of the thinking, conceptions, and opinions that you are constructing and holding, then space opens. Then what seemed small becomes quite wide.

Food offers another interesting image. We all have many different kinds of hunger—material hunger, emotional hunger, spiritual hunger—and there are different kinds of food to satisfy all those different kinds of hungers. Many times in Zen stories the image of food also represents practice or dharma or teaching. A story tells of a monk who said to Chao-chou (Joshu; Joju), "I've just entered your monastery. Please give me your teaching." Chao-chou responded with a question, "Did you eat breakfast?" When the monk answered, "Yes, I did," Chao-chou told him, "Wash your bowl." At that moment, the monk got enlightened.

In another story involving food, a monk came to call on Tan-hsia (Tanka; Dan Ha), who asked, "Where are you coming from?" The monk said, "I come from down the mountain." "Where are you coming from?" is a challenge, meaning, Please show me where your being at this moment is coming from. But the monk answered in the literal way. Now maybe he was a ripe old practitioner, who clearly had attained ordinary, everyday mind; or maybe he was quite new and didn't get the point of the question. So Tan-hsia then asked, "Did you eat yet?" Tan-hsia was not primarily interested in whether this guy had had his lunchtime bowl of rice. He was asking, Has the dharma filled your being, and have you assimilated and digested it? If you have, please show me—show me your practice here and now. The monk's "Yes, I did" was a poor answer; it made yes-versus-no and did not demonstrate the living vitality of his practice. Tan-hsia then asked, "Did the one who gave you food have eyes or not?" meaning: The teacher who gave you the teaching that you ate, was he keen-eyed? Was he a sharp Zen master or not? Because you appear to be a country bumpkin.

When San-sheng said, "I wonder what the golden fish who has passed through the net uses for food," he was asking what kind of practice that person was engaged in, if he was free and had already passed through, and in what way would the free person manifest his or her freedom in the world. Hsueh-feng replied, "When you pass through the net, I'll tell you."

That response is in the style of dharma combat. Rather than giving an answer, Hsueh-feng throws the issue back at the questioner. In *The*

Blue Cliff Record cases, the compiler sometimes adds footnotes after each sentence. They are like little heckles and jibes. After the sentence where Hsueh-feng says, "When you come out of the net, I'll tell you," the commentator writes, "He diminishes the other man's reputation quite a bit."[2] That means, You're not free, so why bother with this question? But San-sheng was already quite confident in himself. He was a successor of Lin-chi, and by that time his mind was clear, so he was not put off by Hsueh-feng's attacks. He replied, "You are the teacher of fifteen hundred people, and you do not even understand the point of my question." Hsueh-feng just responded in a low-key, ordinary way, "This old monk is busy taking care of the temple."

Because Chinese characters have many nuances of meaning, these last lines have been translated in a number of ways. According to one translation, San-sheng said, "The teacher of fifteen hundred people, and you don't even know what to say!" to which Hsueh-feng replied, "My affairs as abbot are many and complicated."[3] According to another translation, San-sheng said, "The renowned teacher of fifteen hundred monks cannot find even one word to say about this topic," and Hsueh-feng answered, "I am the chief abbot and have much to attend to."[4]

Through these, you get the flavor of the dharma combat. But sometimes people take Hsueh-feng's response, "This old monk is busy taking care of the temple," as an apology, as if he were saying, "Well, you know I am not so sharp in dharma combat these days because I am busy taking care of the temple. My duties as abbot are many and complicated, so please excuse me." But actually his response may best be described in Zen language as "within the sheep's skin, lions's claws lie hidden."

What does Hsueh-feng's response, "This old monk is busy taking care of the temple," really mean? To take care of something is to see its value and attend to it. In yoga schools, you often hear that the body is the temple of the spirit, so you should take care of it. But it is not just the body that is the temple. Hsueh-feng once said to the assembly, "This whole universe is the eye of the Buddha; where will you take a crap?"

"This old monk is busy taking care of the temple" means, My practice is to act with caring moment by moment by moment. To act with caring means to respect each and every thing, each and every living being, each and every person, each rock, each tree, the air, the water, everything. Taking care of the temple means expressing care toward each thing. This is the heart of the bodhisattva path.

Once a student came for an interview and told me she was worrying about things, nonstop. I made this suggestion to her: "You should practice by repeating the name of the Bodhisattva of Compassion, Kwan Seum Bosal (Kuan-yin; Kannon). The way you express your worry is by constantly talking to yourself, worrying about this, worrying about that, and driving yourself crazy, so you need an antidote that is also talking. Over and over again repeat, 'Kwan Seum Bosal,' and ask yourself, Who is the one practicing that? Make that your concern."

If you think about it, worry itself is a form of caring, because you don't worry about anything you don't care about. In that sense, the energy of worrying is already connected with the bodhisattva spirit of caring and compassion. The problem is that this form of caring is mixed with fear and self-centeredness. The Heart Sutra says that when the Bodhisattva of Great Compassion perceived that all formations were empty of self-nature, she was freed of all hindrances and fears. Likewise, when we perceive that all things are interconnected, and that our being and everybody else's are dependent on one another, then we become caring and careful in a wide-open manner, rather than in a worrisome, small way. It is important that we all take up Hsueh-feng's practice and his message, and that we too take care of the temple. In that spirit, when you do something you will completely do it, with whole-heartedness and sincerity, and without worrying, checking, or evaluating.

Notes

1. See Seung Sahn, trans., *The Blue Cliff Record* (Cumberland, RI: Kwan Um School of Zen, 1983), 41.

2. Thomas Cleary and J. C. Cleary, trans., *The Blue Cliff Record* (Boston: Shambhala, 1992), 290.

3. Ibid.

4. Katsuki Sekida, trans., *Two Zen Classics: Mumonkan and Hekiganroku* (New York: Weatherhill, 1977), 282.

CHAPTER II

Ho-shan's Knowing How to Hit the Drum

....

*Mountain is cloud, cloud is mountain. This is according to the
formulation of the Heart Sutra, which says, "Form is emptiness,
emptiness is form."*

*Mountain never says, "I'm mountain." Cloud never says,
"I'm cloud." All designations, all labels, are made by thinking.
If you cut off attachment to all thinking, then there is no form
and no emptiness.*

*Mountain is mountain. Cloud is cloud. Form is form.
Emptiness is emptiness. All things, just as they are, are pure
and clear from the very beginning. If you say these three are
correct, the Zen stick will hit you. If you say they are incorrect,
the stick will also hit you. Why?*

Haahh!!

How wonderful—blue mountain puts on a white cloud hat.

....

At the heart of this kong-an is the practice of living in moment time
as a helping being, existing in the world without clinging and without
rejecting. The case appears as number 44 in *The Blue Cliff Record* and
is entitled "Ho-shan's Knowing How to Hit the Drum."

Zen Master Ho Shan, instructing, said, "Studying is called listening. Cutting off study is called nearness. Past these two is true passing.

A monk came forward and asked, "What is true passing?"

Ho Shan said, "Knowing how to hit the drum."

Again he asked, "And what is real truth?"

Ho Shan said, "Knowing how to hit the drum."

Again he asked, "'Mind is Buddha'—I'm not asking about this. What is no mind, no Buddha?"

Ho Shan said, "Knowing how to hit the drum."

Again he asked, "And when a transcendent person comes, how do you receive him?"

Ho Shan said, "Knowing how to hit the drum."[1]

Zen Master Seung Sahn comments:

> Put down all of your speech and thinking. If you are checking, this checking will kill you. Did you hear Ko Sahn's sound of a drum? How many pounds is it? If you know that, you become Buddha's teacher.[2]

Ho-shan (Kasan; Ko Sahn) lived from 891 to 960. When he was seven years old, he left his home and family and went to live in the monastery of the great Chinese Zen Master Hsueh-feng (Seppo; Seol Bong). At that time, Hsueh-feng was already in his mid-seventies and was famous throughout China. It is said he had an assembly of fifteen hundred monks living with him.

Ho-shan remained at the monastery after Hsueh-feng passed away. When he came of age, he took the full monk's precepts. Then he left and began to travel around, looking for another teacher. He eventually came to the monastery of Chiu-feng (Kyuho), who asked him two questions: "Have you seen any realm that can be cultivated?" and "By what shortcut can you get out?"

In the first question, Zen Master Chiu-feng is testing young Ho-shan to see how clear he is about the idea of cultivation. It is a topic discussed by Zen Master Seung Sahn in *The Compass of Zen*, citing a teaching based on Hwa Yen philosophy that says, "It is already apparent in all things. So, without cultivation, you are already complete."[3] Without doing anything—without cultivating any kind of practice—from the beginning you are already complete.

If you can practice using that point as your basic orientation, then that is the shortcut by which to get out, because you perceive that you were never tied up and bound in the first place. You never left your original home.

Ho-shan replied, "In the dark empty clearing, the blind are blind of themselves." Chiu-feng did not approve of that. Ho-shan's reply was somewhat conceptual and attached to the image of emptiness. Chiu-feng said, "No, that's not it." Ho-shan practiced diligently. After some time, he understood Chiu-feng's intent. Suddenly all his knowledge and views dropped away, and he had an awakening experience.

Later, when he was given authorization to teach on his own, Ho-shan—his name actually means Mount Ho—went to Mount Ho and began to teach. A large group of monks gradually gathered on the mountain, and it became a famous teaching center.

Once, the emperor called Ho-shan to the palace for an audience. The emperor asked, "Where are you coming from?" Ho-shan answered, "From Ho-shan (from Mount Ho)." The emperor then asked, "Where is the mountain now?" The emperor must have known a little about Zen language: His first question is a Zen challenge, and the second is a testing question. Ho-shan answered by saying, "The person has come to the palace for an audience, but the mountain has never moved." This means that in all our comings and goings, in all our fluctuations, there is always one thing that is never moving.

But if you think there is some entity there that never moves, that is not quite in accord with Zen teaching. To say that the mountain has never moved, even though the person has come and gone, means that in the midst of our comings and goings, in the midst of our thinking, feeling, and activity, some aspect of us is always steady, always quiet, always stable, and not in turmoil. It is like observing that water changes to steam, steam changes to ice, ice changes to water, but H_2O

is never changing. But there is no H_2O that you could find separate from water, steam, and ice. There is no entity you can find that is not moving; you will only find the quality of not-movingness in the midst of moving.

You can look at the kong-an as having two sections: First, Ho-shan lays out a threefold teaching; second, he gives a living, vital demonstration of what he has taught in the first part.

The teaching says that studying is called listening. Then, cutting off study is called nearness. And finally, past these two is true passing. So first there is something he calls listening, and then something he calls nearness.

This is similar to the teaching in the Heart Sutra: "Form is emptiness, emptiness is form." That is the first designation. But if form is truly emptiness and emptiness is truly form, then you cannot say anything about form, and you cannot say anything about emptiness. So the second designation is "no form, no emptiness," the complete realization of no form, no emptiness. If you do not cling to no form, no emptiness, then each thing, just as it is, becomes clear, so form is just form, emptiness is just emptiness.

The mantra at the end of the Heart Sutra says, "*Gate, gate, paragate, parasamgate, bodhi svaha.*" Loosely translated this means, "Gone, gone, completely gone, completely gone beyond." This is the mantra that reveals the wisdom of gone beyond. *Bodhi* means "wisdom." So "gone beyond" means the transcendence of all opposites, rather than being aloof and above everything, as if floating in the sky.

Zen Master Lin-chi (Rinzai) also had a teaching formulation. While the Heart Sutra's formulation sounds a little philosophical and impersonal, Lin-chi's teaching was more about personal practice. He said, "Sometimes I cut off the subject but leave the object. Sometimes I cut off the object but leave the subject. Sometimes both subject and object are cut off. And sometimes neither subject nor object is cut off." Let's look at these statements.

Sometimes I cut off the subject but leave the object: We all have a tendency to color what we experience with some subjective point of view or frame of reference. If you can cut off that subjectifying quality, each thing becomes clear in its true suchness. This is some-times called the great mirror mind because, just like a mirror, you do not color anything but just reflect it.

Sometimes I cut off the object but leave the subject: Likewise, we relate to the world we are embedded in as if it were separate from us. We keep it at arm's length, so to speak. We make an object that is out there. Here Lin-chi says that sometimes he cuts off the object—the tendency to objectify—but leaves the subject. This means, I leave the sense of one unified being, one complete fabric.

In my first private interview with Zen Master Seung Sahn, he put down his Zen stick and said, "You and the Zen stick, are they the same or different?" I said, "Yes, that's just my problem." When I met him I had already been practicing meditation for ten years, and I was fairly proficient in the formalities, but I always had a subtle feeling that I and my experience were somehow separate: You're over there and I'm over here, and don't come too close.

I told him, "I always feel that I'm a little separate from what I'm relating to." He said, "You ask me the same question." So I said, "You and the Zen stick, are they the same or different?" He immediately hit the floor. I thought that was so absurd and profound at the same time that I burst out laughing. He had to wait while I composed myself to go on with his teaching. Seung Sahn Soen Sa Nim was making the same point as Lin-chi: When you do not make your experience into an object, then there is one unified being.

Sometimes both subject and object are cut off: then nothing. No thing. Also no words, no speech, no names, no forms, so to say any-thing about it misrepresents the point. Zen Master Yun-men said, "Nothing is better than a good thing."

And if you have digested those three, then there is no need to cut off anything. So sometimes neither subject nor object are cut off. At that point, the person exists in the world without clinging and with-out rejecting. So clear compassionate involvement and activity are possible. I am fully in the world, and the world is in me. There is no hesitancy in being fully in the world, and there is also no fear of letting the world into me.

Here Ho-shan says, "Studying is called listening." This means that when we first start to practice, we pay attention, we listen intently, we cultivate awareness, we inquire, we look into our experience. Our study still has a feeling of "I'm doing this, I'm cultivating practice, I'm listening." There is a subtle conceptual kink to it. So he says, "Cutting off study is called nearness."

A monk asked Zen Master Yun-men, "What is the straight way to Yun-men Mountain?" Yun-men immediately gave one of his one-word answers: *Chin*, which in Chinese means "intimacy." Intimacy is the straight way. Intimacy is Yun-men Mountain. Intimacy is the path. Intimacy is the fruition of the path.

When Zen Master Fa-yen (Hogen; Poep An) was still an itinerant monk, he came to Ti Tsang monastery and had an audience with the abbot, who said to him, "What is the meaning of your traveling?" Fa-yen said, "I don't know." Then the abbot said, "Don't-know is closest to it. Not knowing is most intimate." When you have complete don't-know, then that is nearness, that is intimacy, that is closeness. You and everything become one.

Then Ho-shan has a third formulation: Past these two (study and nearness) is called true passing. True passing means to see clearly, hear clearly, act clearly. To act clearly is the great function, the great bodhisattva way, acting in the world in a compassionate and engaged way.

In the second half of the kong-an, Ho-shan reveals through his own activity what he means by true passing. When the monk comes forward and asks, "Zen Master, what is true passing?" Ho-shan answers, "Knowing how to hit the drum." Then:

> What is real truth?
> Knowing how to hit the drum.
> What is no mind, no Buddha?
> Knowing how to hit the drum.
> When a transcendent man comes, how do you receive
> him?
> Knowing how to hit the drum.

This style is sometimes referred to as flavorless speech, colorless words. There is nothing philosophical or conceptual in it. There is only Ho-shan revealing himself and his functioning through the phrase, "Knowing how to hit the drum." *Boom!* Do you want to know what true passing is? Knowing how to hit the drum.

Ho-shan is a boring fellow in a way—tenacious but boring—because he uses the same phrase four times. I can imagine that monk challenging him and saying, "But Zen Master, you only use one device. Don't you know anything else?" Then I can picture Ho-shan replying, "Oh yes, I know something else that is very different from this." "Then what is it?" "Knowing how to hit the drum." Because that "knowing how to hit the drum" is not the same as the previous "knowing how to hit the drum," which is not the same as the one before that, and not the same as the one before that, any more than our meditation practice today is the same as our sitting practice yesterday or the day before. Yet we sit down in the same way every day. We cross our legs in the same way every day. We assume the same posture each time in the same way. But it is not the same.

Once a student who was the Zen Center's head dharma teacher was going through a hard time. The job of head dharma teacher had begun to feel stale and tedious. He said to me, "You don't have to be a rocket scientist to be the head dharma teacher."

Well, you don't have to be a rocket scientist to be the Zen master, either! Nor do you have to be a rocket scientist to be a beginning student who has clear beginner's mind. It is not important to be a rocket scientist or to be highly inventive. What is most important is not to lose the true spirit of repetition, and that is what Ho-shan demonstrates through his "knowing how to hit the drum." It is important as we proceed with our practice and with nurturing this way of life and path that we not lose the true spirit of repetition. We must see that today is not the same as yesterday, even though it appears to be exactly the same.

Although the phrase "knowing how to hit the drum" is not conceptual or intellectual or philosophical, there is still something connoted in that phrase, something about action and about the moment. If you look at the vocabulary of Zen and Buddhism, you can see that it is oriented toward action, even though it might not appear so. We use words like *path*, *way*, or *vehicle*: the Eightfold Path, the Middle Way, and the Great Vehicle. These are all action words.

Essentially Zen practice is not about cultivating quietism. If you look at the way we practice sitting meditation, it is not oriented toward withdrawing and becoming quiet; it is an activity that we engage in. We sit with full awareness; we take charge of our bodies; we pay attention; and we enter into that fully, moment by moment by moment. It is much more an activity and an action than a withdrawal, even though you may feel a certain sense of quietude and stability while practicing. And if you look at the language of Zen kong-ans and dharma combat, you will see that the response to a question will often be in some kind of dynamic form, like hitting the floor, or shouting.

If you can digest and assimilate and make yours the experience of just mirroring without subjectifying or coloring; if you can digest and assimilate the experience of not objectifying, just feeling the solidarity and equality of all things and you together; and if you can let go of the concept of I and the concept of this world, then you can reveal that attainment through clear, alive, and vital action. Then subject and object, inside and outside, visible and invisible, all become one unity. This is the realization and the expression of the dynamic principle that is at the root of our existence. Sometimes this is referred to as, Just do it! There is nothing high-fallutin' about it—just do it. That is moment mind, acting without coloration of past and future.

With just this moment, you perceive the past as a present activity. In doing so, you become free of the binding quality of the past. To perceive the past as an activity in this moment means that this moment is the experience of remembrance. If you anticipate or project, then that is the future *in this moment*. Remembrance is an activity just now. Projection or anticipation is an activity just now.

This experience is alluded to in one version of the story of Buddha's enlightenment. It says that while Buddha was sitting under the bodhi tree, he perceived the whole interlocking net of causes, effects, and conditions, what traditional Buddhism calls the chain of dependent origination. He perceived this in the moment and became awakened to the unity of all things.

Ho-shan says, "Knowing how to hit the drum." There is just *Boom!* and gone. Again, *Boom!* and gone. That is moment mind, or moment world. No before, no after, just that moment—*Boom!* Then gone completely.

Notes

1. See Seung Sahn, trans., *The Blue Cliff Record* (Cumberland, RI: Kwan Um School of Zen, 1983), 37.
2. Seung Sahn, *The Whole World Is a Single Flower* (Rutland, VT: Tuttle, 1992), 211.
3. Seung Sahn, *The Compass of Zen* (Boston: Shambhala, 1997), 320.

CHAPTER 12

Jui-yen Calls, "Master!"

If you understand THIS, then you understand the place where your mind's original home is and you can meet your original master face-to-face.

If you attain THIS, then all thinking, all words, all designations are completely cut off. At that point, there is no mind, no master, nothing at all. If originally nothing, where do the sun, moon, and stars come from?

If you do not attach or cling to nothing, then your eyes see clearly, clear listening is also possible, and everything that is just in front of you is your true master.

But that is only a good idea. What is the realization of it?

Look!!

The wall is white, the floor beneath you is brown.

"Original master" is a theme that appears in case 12 of the *Wu-men-kuan* (*Mumonkan; Mu Mun Kwan*), "Jui-yen Calls, 'Master.'" Here is the case and the poem connected to it:

Jui-yen used to call to himself every day, "Master!" He would answer, "Yes?"

"Keep clear."

"Yes."

"Never be deceived by others any place, any time."

"Yes, yes."[1]

That is the case itself. In the poem after it, Zen Master Wu-men says:

> Students of the Way do not understand truth;
> They only understand consciousness.
> The cause of life and death through infinite kalpas,
> Ignorant people call it original man.[2]

In the first two lines, Wu-men asserts that we confuse our discriminating consciousness with our original self. Then, in that confusion, we become lost and get caught up in birth and death. Wu-men also makes a comment after the case:

> Old Jui-yen buys and sells himself. He brings forth lots
> of angel faces and demon masks and plays with them.
> Why? *Look!* One kind calls, one kind answers, one kind
> is aware, one kind will not be deceived by others. If you
> still cling to understanding, you're in trouble. If you try
> to imitate Jui-yen, your discernment is altogether that
> of a fox.[3]

Wu-men's comment urges us to recognize the difference between superficially imitating or repeating something and going to the heart of the matter, really grasping the spirit of it. You could think about it this way: Someone says such and such poem is one that you should really know. One person picks up the poem, reads it superficially, and feels no real connection with it. Yet someone else reads it and feels a deep, heartfelt connection. Both are essentially following someone else's suggestion, but the connection is entirely different.

Zen Master Seung Sahn also has a comment on the case:

Stupid, stupid! Woman's face, man's face, who understands?

Wash your face, then it appears clearly.[4] ["Appears clearly" *is* master.]

There is a traditional saying: Just seeing is buddha nature. It does not say you will see buddha nature but that the very act of just seeing is itself the manifestation of buddha nature, or awakened mind.

Jui-yen (Zuigan; Song Am) was a Zen master who lived between 800 and 900. He studied with two major Zen masters—the great Yen-t'ou (Ganto; Am Du) and Chia-shan (Kassan). Not much is known about Jui-yen's practice history or where he came from, but there is a record of his first meeting with Yen-t'ou and his first meeting with Chia-shan.

At Jui-yen's first meeting with Yen-t'ou, he asked, "What is the fundamental constant principle?" Yen-t'ou replied, "Moving." In that one word, Yen-t'ou revealed the fundamental and eternal principle, but Jui-yen did not get it. So he said, "What is this *moving*?" Yen-t'ou replied, "Can't you see the eternal and fundamental principle?" Jui-yen stood thinking. Then Yen-t'ou said, "If you agree to this, then you are still caught up in the dust of the world, and if you disagree with this, you will always be sunk in birth and death."[5] Jui-yen was bewildered. Essentially, agreeing and disagreeing are ten thousand miles from the revelation of this one word, *moving*.

Later Jui-yen practiced with Chia-shan. Two interesting stories are told about this Zen master. Once Chia-shan was sitting meditation with Zen Master Tung-shan (Tozan; Dong Sahn), who came to him and said, "How is it?" Chia-shan replied, "Just like this." That is an important statement. How is your meditation? How is your practice? How is it? Just like this.

Another story tells of one of Chia-shan's students, who traveled widely, calling on various other Zen masters. Yet, in all those different temples and assemblies, he found nothing that he considered particularly deep or enlightening. Whenever he arrived at a new temple, the Zen master would ask, "Where are you coming from?" The student would reply, "I've come from Chia-shan." Then the Zen master would say, "Oh, Chia-shan is a great and profound teacher. He has an extremely subtle understanding of the Zen Dharma." After a while, the student began to think, Maybe I missed something when I was there with Chia-shan. He turned around and went back to Chia-shan's temple.

Once there, he said to Chia-shan, "You have an extremely profound and subtle understanding of the teaching. Why did you never reveal it to me when I was with you?" Chia-shan asked, "What are you talking about? When you cooked the rice, didn't I light the match? When you carried the pail with the rice in it, didn't I also hold up my bowl to you? When did I ever betray your expectation?" At that the monk had an awakening.[6] That was Chia-shan's style—very subtle, without much drama.

When Jui-yen first met him, Chia-shan asked, "Where are you coming from?" Jui-yen replied, "I've come from Lying Dragon Mountain." This was the mountain on which Yen-t'ou's temple was located. Then Chia-shan said, "When you left there, did the dragon rise up?" The name Lying Dragon Mountain suggests spiritual power in potential form: lying asleep like a great mountain. But "did the dragon rise up?" means, How is your spiritual power functioning? Jui-yen just looked around. At that Chia-shan said, "That's like applying burning moxa to cure skin that has already been burnt."

Moxa is a Chinese medicine made of dried herbs that can be burned over acupuncture points to effect certain kinds of cures. Chia-shan was telling Jui-yen that he totally missed it. But Jui-yen held his own and replied, "Why do you, Master, undergo that kind of torture?" meaning, It's not me who is mistaken, but you. Chia-shan just kept silent. At that point, Jui-yen probably thought, This teacher is not so strong. So he said to Chia-shan, "Suchness is easy. Not-suchness is difficult. In suchness, you can see clearly. If you are in not-suchness, then you're in emptiness. Where are you just now, Teacher?" Chia-shan responded, "Today you've made a fool of this old monk." Jui-yen had been caught in the net at that moment, but he did not realize it until years later.[7]

Toward the end of Jui-yen's dialogue with himself in the kong-an we are considering, he says, "Never be deceived by others." His original teacher, Yen-t'ou, had a saying, "I never deceive myself." Chia-shan says, "Today you made a fool of me." If you are deceived by someone, then you have been made a fool of. Somehow the notion of deception must have made a strong impression on Jui-yen.

The case begins, "Jui-yen used to call to himself every day, 'Master!' He would answer, 'Yes?'" Just about everyone smiles the first time they hear this; we all can recognize the experience of talking to ourselves. People who are a little more eccentric than the norm talk to themselves a little more, and sometimes out loud. There is a certain humor here and also a slightly irrational quality.

Once, as a student entered the gate, Zen Master Hsueh-feng (Seppo; Seol Bong) suddenly pushed the student over, shoved him to the ground, and demanded, "What is this?" The student immediately had a vivid awakening experience and, forgetting himself, got up, raised up his arms, and started dancing around. Hsueh-feng said, "Are you behaving rationally?" The student replied, "What has rationality got to do with this?" Hsueh-feng stroked the student's back a few times and confirmed his experience. Like Jui-yen's calling and answering himself, it was not exactly rational behavior.

Whenever Zen Master Seung Sahn talked about this case, he made two essential points: First, Jui-yen has a very simple mind; he generates only two minds. Most of us generate many different kinds: pain mind, sad mind, anger mind, sex mind, food mind, money mind, success mind, failure mind. But Jui-yen generates only calling mind and answering mind. If those two become one, there is no mind, no master. That means there is nothing I. If there is nothing I, then there is no consciousness that clouds seeing, hearing, feeling, or acting. Everything becomes correct master at that point.

Second, Jui-yen is like a child. As children, we all had conversations with ourselves. Think about how a child will pick up a doll and start talking to it, getting engrossed in the conversation, even though the doll is not really saying anything back. That does not seem to faze the child at all; he keeps talking and playing with the doll. It has a quality of innocence and simplicity. In Zen, we call that play samadhi. Jui-yen makes two and then plays. He makes calling master and answering master, but where do those two come from? And which of the two is the correct master? Those are among a number of questions suggested by this case. When Jui-yen calls to himself, what is self? What is Jui-yen's self? What is myself? What is yourself? When he says, "Master!" what is master? And what about his response, "Yes?"

We can get some understanding of the notion of original master from other stories, as well. In one, a visiting monk said to Zen Master Shih-hu, "I've just entered your monastery, please give me some pointers." Shih Hu said, "Before you entered my monastery, I'd already given you some pointers." The monk then asked, "How am I to understand that?" Shih Hu told him, "Understanding is not necessary." That is original master. When he tells him there is no need to understand, he is saying that the true master, the true teaching, is not going to be found in your understanding; it is to be found in your not understanding and not knowing.[8]

In a similar story, a monk asked Zen Master Chen-sui, "What are the very first words?" Chen-sui said, "The master was already here even before the world had formed." Both stories are teachings about original master. Before the world formed is not necessarily some ancient eon millions of years ago. The world forms in our experience each and every moment. We generate form moment by moment by moment and create our own version of the world. But even before we do that forming, something called master is already present. Master means some fundamental ruling principle. What is the ruling principle of this body and mind? That is master, and the subject of Jui-yen's kong-an. The answer he gives himself, "Yes?" is also master, because in that one word he manifests the spirit of openness, responsiveness, and readiness that is sometimes called "standing on the edge, ready to leap."

An incident back when the Chogye International Zen Center of New York was fairly new will help explain that idea. One student wanted us to have a seven-day retreat—something we had never done. The student was dedicated to the idea, so he organized a small group of people who would commit to practicing. Then we asked

Zen Master Seung Sahn if he would be willing to come and lead the retreat. He said yes. At that time, he did not care if there were going to be ten people sitting or a hundred. If there were a few people who had sincere interest, then he was willing to come.

The schedule for a retreat day begins with 108 bows, then sitting meditation, with individual interviews given. After that we would have chanting meditation. Usually the Zen master would still be upstairs finishing interviews when we started chanting. One morning, about five minutes after chanting practice had begun, Zen Master Seung Sahn suddenly appeared in the dharma room in his underwear, dancing around wildly. One student who was close with him thought he had completely lost his mind, so the student stood up and tried to restrain him. Seung Sahn gave him a quick karate kick and knocked him over. When things had settled down, Seung Sahn explained the meaning of his action. He put it in traditional Korean terms, so I have to make a slight cultural translation here, but this was essentially what he said: "When I came down from the interview room and heard the way you were chanting, it sounded as if you were all half asleep. I was concerned that in your half sleep state 'demons' were going to enter your consciousnesses, so I knew I had to arouse your energy quickly. So this occurred." That is the spirit of Yes—being able to respond freely to different situations, not for oneself but for all beings.

Immediately after he calls out "Master!" and answers "Yes?" Jui-yen says, "You must keep clear," then, "Yes!" Keeping clear is the ongoing practice of not obscuring what is right in front of us. Everybody has to practice that—beginning students and experienced students have to practice this over and over again. Even great Zen masters, after some profound enlightenment, still have to practice keeping clear. So Jui-yen answers, "Yes."

Then he says one more thing: "Never be deceived by others any place, any time." That statement has two essential meanings. First, it suggests the question, Can you remain steady and not be pulled out from your centeredness by things that are going on around you? That requires a particular kind of practice: On the one hand, it does not mean to block out everything that anyone else is doing, because that contradicts the spirit of Yes. On the other hand, if you lose yourself to everything that is going on, then that is a problem.

Many times you see that latter difficulty in groups where people come and practice together or even live and practice together. Doing this kind of practice is not so easy, because the activity of keeping clear means that I form an intention to continue, day in and day out, to practice in this way and to be steady and consistent. In a group like that—where there is a formal structure to the practice, where things are done at certain times—sometimes one person always comes late. Then some other person only stays for the sitting and never for the chanting. Other people see that happening, and their minds begin to move. Initially their determination and direction were clear, but they begin to think, I don't like chanting so much; I don't know what the words mean and don't get the point of this.

When that happens, you begin to lose the clarity of your original intention; you get caught up in like and dislike and pay attention to what someone else is doing, ignoring what your clear original master has pointed to. This is when you begin to be deceived by others. It is important to recognize how that emerges and to avoid getting pulled into it. Should you find yourself getting pulled in, you must be able to come back to your original practice intention, like a compass needle pointing straight north.

Not being deceived by others, however, is more than not getting pulled in; it also implies a certain confidence and at the same time a certain openness.

If you stay open and say yes, even an insult is no problem. That is also, Don't be deceived by others. Can you keep your own center? Koun Yamada Roshi, a twentieth-century Japanese Zen master, says, "Even though Shakyamuni Buddha may come and say, 'You are wrong,' or 'Your enlightenment is not true,' you should not be confused but should rely on your realization."[9]

The second point here is that, from the most fundamental standpoint, as soon as you generate the concept of other versus self, you are holding the world at arm's length. And in that moment you create a deception by forming an idea of other over there and me over here.

Zen Master Man Gong has a couple of short poems about this. The first one is titled, "The Prajna Ship":

> Everything is impermanent, but there is truth.
> You and I are not two, not one:
> Only your stupid thinking is nonstop.
> Already alive in the Prajna ship.[10]

The commentary says:

> What do you see now? What do you hear now? Every-
> thing appears clearly in front of you.[11]

The second line, "You and I are not two, not one," speaks to the same point as Jui-yen's "Never be deceived by others." The next line, "Only your stupid thinking is nonstop," refers to the continual generating of delusion and confusion: seeing things in terms of self and other, inside and outside, and not perceiving the clarity of not two, not one.

Then the last line, "Already alive in the Prajna [wisdom] ship": The Prajna Paramita Sutra ends with the mantra, "*Gate gate paragate parasamgate bodhi svaha*," which means, "Wisdom that is revealed by going completely beyond." *Gate* means "gone," so literally it is saying, Gone, gone, gone beyond, completely gone beyond, *bodhi* (awakened wisdom). If you completely go beyond any notion of self and other, two or one, inside or outside, then you are already alive in the ship of wisdom. So don't hold anything; completely let go and recognize your original aliveness.

The second poem by Man Gong says:

> Holding a bamboo stick, never stop.
> Already arrive in front of Bo Dok cave.
> Who is the host, who is guest? They cannot see each
>   other.
> Only very close by, the gurgle of the stream.[12]

The commentary states:

The sound of the stream takes away both guest and host.[13]

I hope we can all practice this Zen of not two, not one, and let the gurgle of the stream and the sound of the car horns in the street, as well as everything else we experience, take away the dichotomy of host and guest, self and other. If that happens, you can help yourself and others without being deceived.

Notes

1. See Seung Sahn, trans., *The Mu Mun Kwan* (Cumberland, RI: Kwan Um School of Zen, 1983), 14.
2. Ibid.
3. Robert Aitken, trans., *The Gateless Barrier* (San Francisco: North Point Press, 1991), 81.
4. Seung Sahn, *The Whole World Is a Single Flower* (Rutland, VT: Tuttle, 1992), 181.
5. See Thomas Cleary, trans., *Book of Serenity* (Boston: Shambhala, 1988), 316.
6. See Frederick Franck, ed., *Zen and Zen Classics: Selections from R. H. Blyth.* (New York: Vintage, 1978), 236.
7. See Katsuki Sekida, trans., *Two Zen Classics: Mumonkan and Hekiganroku* (New York: Weatherhill, 1977), 53–54.
8. See C. M. Chen, *The Lighthouse in the Ocean of Ch'an* (Carmel, NY: Buddhist Assn. of the United States, 1996), 34.
9. Koun Yamada, trans., *The Gateless Gate* (Boston: Wisdom, 2004), 65.
10. Seung Sahn, *Whole World,* 106.
11. Ibid.
12. Ibid., 107.
13. Ibid.

CHAPTER 13

Yun-men's Bell Sound and Seven-Fold Robe

*A student asked an old master, "In this world of coming and going,
how can we be free and unfettered?" The master immediately retorted,
"Who has ever put you in chains?"*

That being so, where do ideas of freedom and bondage come from?

*If you attain that point, then how will you use it freely and constructively
in the world?*

Haahh!!

A dog understands a dog's job. A cat understands a cat's job.

Do you understand your job?

Case 16 in the *Wu-men-kuan* (*Mumonkan; Mu Mun Kwan*) collection,
"Yun-men's Bell Sound and Seven-Fold Robe," recalls a brief speech
given by Zen Master Yun-men (Ummon; Un Mun):

Yun-men said, "The world is vast and wide; why do you put on
a seven-fold robe at the sound of the bell?"[1]

That was the whole talk. Then he got down from his high seat and
went back to his room.

In this short discourse, there is something about freedom and constraint, the absolute and the relative, the noumenal and the phenomenal, and how these all come together.

The notion of freedom in Zen is a little different from certain other notions of freedom we sometimes hold or indulge in, for instance, the freedom to be yourself, or the freedom of getting away from something, or the freedom of creative expression, such as the grace and elegance of a ballet dancer.

But if you watch a ballet class, you can see that it is extremely rigorous in its demands. Similarly you might think about the freedom attained in martial arts training, the free-flowing movement in t'ai chi or kung fu. But if you attend a t'ai chi or kung fu class, you will be asked to pay almost obsessive attention to each detail, and you may find it extremely constraining. Yet out of those demanding situations comes a creative freedom of movement. So there are many different approaches to freedom.

Recently I saw one of those television commercials where you are not sure what is being advertised. Usually there is some eroticism in the tone and maybe a slightly surreal image. They are trying to get your attention more than anything else. In this one, a young woman says, "I do what I want. I can't do anything else." That is her notion of freedom. But if I can't do anything else, is that freedom or constraint? It's not so clear.

The kong-an tells of putting on a robe, but before we get into that, here is a little freedom story about taking off a robe: A nun came to the Zen master and asked, "What is dharma?" [What is truth, what is the true way?] The Zen master said, "No hindrance." The nun asked, "Then what does 'no hindrance' mean?" The Zen master replied, "Why do you wear clothes?" At this, the nun stripped naked and walked to the door.[2]

It is clear that the nun understood the freedom of taking it all off and throwing it away, but it is not so clear that she understood the freedom of putting it back on and walking freely in the world. The point there is similar to the point in this kong-an.

Yun-men was born in 864 CE. He became a monk when he was in his teens and took his final vows as a monk when he was twenty years old. At first he studied the texts that dealt with monks' discipline. After a while, however, he was not satisfied with these alone. At the age of twenty-five, he made a journey to call on Zen Master Mu-chou (Bokushu; Muk Ju). When it says in these stories that he made a journey, it means he really made a journey. Nowhere was close to anywhere else in China at that time. He probably had to travel hundreds of miles on foot to get to where Mu-chou was living.

Mu-chou had once been the head monk under Zen Master Huang-po (Obaku), but by this time he had returned to his native village to take care of his aging mother and was no longer living as a monk. He lived in a little hut, supporting himself and his mother by making and selling straw sandals. He had a reputation as a recluse who was abrupt and unpredictable.

When Mu-chou saw Yun-men coming, he went into his hut and closed the door. Yun-men came to the door and knocked. Mu-chou said, "Who is it?"

"It's me, Yun-men."

"What do you want?"

"I am not clear about myself and have come for your guidance."

Mu-chou opened the door, looked him up and down, and—closed the door.

The story says this went on for three days. On the third day, as Mu-chou was about to close the door in his face one more time, Yun-men—having more energy by then—shoved his way inside. Immediately Mu-chou grabbed him by the robe and demanded, "Say it! Say it!" Yun-men hesitated. At that point, Mu-chou shoved him out, saying, "Useless stuff!" and closed the door.

The simplest version of the story says that Yun-men attained enlightenment just then. More elaborate versions add drama to the story and even have a certain magical flavor about them. In one, when Mu-chou is about to shove him out the door, Yun-men rallies and sticks his foot in the door so he cannot be totally closed out, but Mu Chou closes the door on his foot. The most extreme version says he breaks his leg, and at that moment Yun-men attains enlightenment. That is pain enlightenment! Some people understand that when they sit a Zen retreat. After several hours, when there is only pain in your legs or only pain in your back, sometimes you can just completely become one with that experience and something opens up for you.

The phrase Mu-chou chooses when he grabs Yun-men and pushes him out is translated into English as "useless stuff," but the Chinese words actually refer to stone drills from the Qin Dynasty. During the Qin Dynasty (221–207 BCE), the emperor wanted to make a rather grand palace. He had some huge stone drills made to help with the excavation and construction. But the project was never realized, and these huge stone drills were left over. That phrase, as an idiom in Chinese, came to mean useless stuff. Those huge stone drills were left over, and you could not do anything with them.

They suggest an interesting question: What kind of stone drills do each of us have left over from some antiquated, grandiose project that we mounted in our mind at some time or other? When we continue to hold unrealistic expectations about such a project or feel disappointment about it, then a remnant of it is still around. That is what Mu-chou calls useless stuff. That is when, in the Zen tradition, we say, "Put it all down."

Some years ago I was in China, attending a conference arranged by the Kwan Um School of Zen. The conference, mostly organized by our group in Hong Kong, was held in Canton Province in southern China, at the Temple of the Sixth Patriarch, in the small city of Shaoguan. There, as in most orthodox monasteries in China, Korea, and other Asian countries, a formal seating arrangement is used at ceremonies. The monks sit in one place, the nuns in another, the laypeople in yet another. In these societies, the highest respect is paid to the monks; nuns are considered second class compared to the monks; and laypeople are in a third class, despite the fact that they are sometimes the big donors who support the whole operation.

Several of us there from the Kwan Um School of Zen had the title of Zen master, but I was the only layperson with that title. Now, you have to understand that in China you do not organize anything without the help of the Communist Party. So invitations for the ceremony had gone out to the minister of Buddhist affairs in Canton Province, to the mayor of Shaoguan, and to other officials. We were told before the conference, which was hosted by a group of very orthodox Chinese monks, that the American and European lay students who attended should wear ties and jackets or dresses or skirts rather than robes during this ceremony.

As it worked out, Zen Master Seung Sahn sat beside an elderly, respected monk who was the abbot of the temple. With them were several American and European monks from our school, along with all the Chinese monks and nuns. In the laypeoples' section, the Communist officials were given front row seats. But nobody knew quite what to do with me, a layman who is a Zen master, so they sat me behind the Communist officials. A member of the Hong Kong sangha, who was acting as a host, came over to apologize for my being seated in the rear. Later she told a friend of mine how appreciative she was because I didn't seem to be bothered much about being seated off to the side. In truth, I was so happy to be at the Sixth Patriarch's temple that the formalities were all secondary. If I have learned anything from all this training, it is, don't carry too much with you.

But let's get back to the story of Yun-men. After his enlightenment experience, he stayed with Mu-chou for about five years. Then Mu-chou suggested that he call on Zen Master Hsueh-feng (Seppo; Seol Bong). Again he set out, traveling to Hsueh-feng's monastery. When Yun-men reached the village at the foot of the mountain—the monastery was up on top—he met another monk. He asked the monk, "Are you traveling up the mountain to the monastery?" The monk said yes. Then Yun-men said to him, "When you get there, I want you to ask Zen Master Hsueh-feng a question, but don't tell him that I said to ask. Say that it's your question."

Soon after the monk reached the monastery, Hsueh-feng came into the hall and mounted the rostrum to answer questions. The visiting monk came forward and followed Yun-men's instruction, saying, "Old fellow, when will you get the yoke off your neck?" Hsueh-feng came down from the high seat, grabbed the monk, and said, "Speak! Speak!" The monk did not know what to say. Hseuh-feng said, "That question is not yours" and pushed him away. But the monk insisted,

"No, no. That's my question." Hseuh-feng called for the attendant and said, "Attendant, bring some rope and some big sticks." When the monk thought he was going to get a beating, he recanted, saying, "A monk down in the village told me to ask that." At that, Hsueh-feng told the assembly, "Go to the village and greet the teacher of five hundred people."

Now Yun-men was not a teacher at that time, just a wandering monk, but he went up the hill to the monastery, where he joined Hsueh-feng's assembly. He did not have any particular position; he was just another monk in the assembly. He stayed there for seven or eight years. Then, in his late thirties, he again set out, traveling all around China for the next ten years. He finally wound up just where we had the aforementioned conference, in the town of Shaoguan in Canton Province. He first visited the temple of the Sixth Patriarch. Then he went to the monastery of Zen Master Rumin.

For many years before Yun-men appeared, Rumin had never appointed a permanent head monk in his assembly. (The head monk is like the second in command and presides over the meditation hall.) But every so often Rumin would make a cryptic remark, saying first, "Now the head monk is being born." Then, a few years later, "Now the head monk is playing with his toys." After a few more years, "Now the head monk is tending the cattle in the field." He went on like this for years.

Then one day he said, "Now the head monk is at the gate," and in came Yun-men. He was given the head monk's seat and stayed in that position for seven or eight years. And when the old abbot died, Yun-men was given that job. So it was not until he was fifty-five that he became a Zen master. He continued to teach there until his death, thirty years later.

For me, the most magical part, the most dramatic part, is not in the events of broken-leg enlightenment or in the Zen master's clair-voyance about the head monk's arrival. What is most magical is the perseverance of this monk Yun-men, who studied for so many years and traveled around China, yet did not assume teaching responsibil-ity until he was fifty-five years old. His example is an incentive for the spirit of practice. It makes us realize that the refinement of maturation goes on over time; it is more important than any particular experience, title, or attainment.

Now we come back to the case: "The world is vast and wide. Why do you put on a seven-fold robe at the sound of the bell?" There are four elements here: the world is vast and wide, the why, the seven-fold robe, and the sound of the bell.

The world is vast and wide. This means that the world of our experience in its original form is open and free; it is a plenum of infinite possibilities. It is an expression representing the absolute.

Why do you put on a seven-fold robe? The seven-fold robe is the monk's outer robe, worn in ceremonies and services. In each corner of the robe is a little square; these represent the four directions of the compass. Then there is the middle point, the zenith at the top, and the nadir at the bottom. There are also a number of lines—seven, or nine, or maybe even sixteen. The lines are the folds, because the cloth is folded up and then sewn.

The robe is a symbolic representation of the world. Its lines, it is sometimes said, represent rows of grain. So when you put on the robe, you take on the whole world and carry it as the field of cultivation of your practice. It is a kind of intention or vow. But essentially, that is nothing new, nothing added, because we are already carrying the whole world with us. When you come to the recognition of the fundamental point, there is no inside, no outside, no subject, no object, no world versus you. You and the world become one. From this point of view, you are already carrying the world, and the world is already carrying you. Out of that spirit comes compassionate activity and a feeling of gratitude.

But here, when Yun-men says, "The world is vast and wide. Why do you put on a seven-fold robe at the sound of the bell?" he is talking to an assembly of monks. They put on their seven-fold robes several times every day, whenever they enter the hall for chanting ceremonies. Early in the morning the bell rings—*ding*—and they put on their seven-fold robes and go in and chant. Then, in late morning, right before the noonday meal, again the bell rings—*ding*—and they put on their seven-fold robes and go in and chant. In the evening, they do the same thing.

For a monk or a nun, there is nothing unusual about that. If Yun-men were living today, he might say, "This world is vast and wide. When the alarm clock rings in the morning, why do you get out of bed?" Or, "This world is vast and wide. Why do you put on a neck-tie and jacket, or a skirt and blouse, and go out to work every day?" Or, "This world is vast and wide. Why do you pick up the telephone when it rings?" He is just making a comment about the interface of openness and freedom and the specificity of moment-by-moment engagement. It would be something like saying, "Ocean, you're so deep and so wide. Why do you have waves?" Or saying to the sky, "You're so vast and open. Why do you have white clouds floating back and forth?"

The *why* means, Don't just do what you do mechanically, without any attentiveness and recognition in your daily activities. *Why* means, Look, look deeply. Why do you put on the seven-fold robe at the sound of the bell? When you do something, really do it completely; be one with it.

In that *why*, we come to a recognition that putting on the seven-fold robe is "the world is vast and wide." And "the world is vast and wide" is putting on the seven-fold robe. When you function one hundred percent when doing something, without thinking—without making divisions of inside and outside, good and bad, before and after—when you completely enter into it with full attentiveness, at that time your activity is the expression of "the world is vast and wide." And the vast world is there at that moment in that particular experience.

Some time ago, I heard of a comment attributed to Igor Stravin-sky. He said that when he sat down at the piano to compose music, the first thing that would hit him—as he sat there, before he started to work—was the immensity of the infinite possibilities of what he might compose. He said that if he had stayed in that state, he would not have been able to write a single note. So he would focus on one small theme. As he worked with that, he said, he would feel as if the energy of the vastness of all the possibilities was flowing through the one theme. That is, "This world is vast and wide. Why do you sit at the piano and write notes on paper?"

> If you attain, all things become one.
> If you do not attain, the ten thousand things become separate.
> If you do not attain, all things become one.
> If you attain, the ten thousand things become clear.[3]

In one particular Buddhist philosophical school, the Hua-yen (Kegon; Hwa-om), they talk about the world of our experience as existing in four different realms: the realm of the absolute, the realm of the phenomenal or relative, the realm where the absolute and the relative interpenetrate, and the realm where all individual phenomena interpenetrate. So you can view your experience from four different perspectives.

That is something like saying, if we use the image of the ocean again, that the realm of the absolute is the depth of the ocean or just the fact of the water there. The relative or the phenomenal is the surface waves. The interpenetration of the absolute and the relative is the fact that every particular wave is expressing the vastness and depth of the ocean. There is no wave apart from the depth of the ocean, and there is no ocean without waves. You cannot talk about an ocean without waves, and you cannot talk about waves without a deep ocean supporting them. So those two interpenetrate, or intersupport, each other. That is the absolute and the relative interpenetrating.

Then there is the fourth aspect. If you look at each wave, you will see that all are interconnected. One wave makes the next wave; that wave makes another wave. Likewise, we are all interpenetrating and supporting each other in some fashion. The rain falls, the ground becomes wet. The sun comes out, the whole earth is bright. I write, so you read. You read, so I write. That is the interbeing of all individual phenomena.

The notion of oneness here is a little different than in certain other traditions. For example, Yun-men once addressed the assembly, saying, "All individual things are essentially without difference, but don't stretch the duck's legs and cut the crane's legs short, don't fill in the valleys and level the peaks, and then think that they're all the same." If you recognize oneness, that does not take away the individual characteristics of any particular being or any particular expression of being. We still, in some sense, retain our unique expressiveness as a particular wave in this ocean. At the same time, we are never separate from the universal absolute._

Wu-men says, in the first line of his poem, "If you attain, all things become one." Some translations say, "If you understand, all things become one." Then, "If you do not attain [or do not understand], the ten thousand things become separate."[4] Those are the first two realms: oneness and separateness.

Then he goes a step further, "If you do not attain, all things become one." That is similar to the Heart Sutra's presentation: "No eyes, no ears, no nose, no tongue, no body, no color, no sound . . . and no attainment, with nothing to attain."

If you perceive no attainment, with nothing to attain, then you perceive that all things, even without your attainment, are already one, all things are already interconnected, your practice or your insight does not make anything become one. It is already existing that way.

Wu-men says, "If you do not attain, all things become one." Or, you could say, if you don't understand, all things become one. If you completely don't know and don't understand, at that time you recognize that all things, from the very first, were already not separate—not one, not two. But truly, you can't even open your mouth to say anything.

So, if you do not attain, all things become one. If you perceive that there is no attainment, with nothing to attain, all things become one.

If you attain, the ten thousand things become clear. If the ten thousand things become clear, then each of us will recognize our responsibility to one another and will manifest some intelligent action to help this world. That is the ultimate direction of our Zen practice and the way of true freedom.

Notes

1. Seung Sahn, trans., *The Mu Mun Kwan* (Cumberland, RI: Kwan Um School of Zen, 1983), 20.
2. Seung Sahn, *The Whole World Is a Single Flower* (Rutland, VT: Tuttle, 1992), 12.
3. Seung Sahn, *Mu Mun Kwan,* 20.
4. See Zenkei Shibayama, *The Gateless Barrier* (Boston: Shambhala, 1974), 122; and Thomas Cleary, trans., *No Barrier* (New York: Bantam, 1993), 81.

CHAPTER 14

Tung-shan's Three Pounds of Flax

*Zen Master Chao-chou would often point the way to students
by exclaiming, "Go drink tea."*

*Zen Master Ho-shan illumined the great function by using the phrase,
"Knowing how to hit the drum."*

*Pointing the way, illuminating the great function, what is it
that these two are getting at?*

Haahh!!

What are you doing now? Listen carefully.

We have seen that many Zen kong-ans use symbolic imagery. For
example, if a master asks a student, "Did you bring your sword?"
essentially he or she is not asking a student about a sword but about
the sharpness of the student's mind. The image of an ox or a rhinoceros is often used to represent mind, and one kong-an introduces the
image of a net. All are metaphoric or symbolic in some way. In this
chapter we look into a kong-an that is completely nonsymbolic. In
the language of Zen, we could say that it is completely tasteless and
colorless. The interchange is brief. It appears in both the *Wu-men-kuan*
(*Mumonkan; Mu Mun Kwan*) and *The Blue Cliff Record*. This kong-an
has been used frequently by Zen masters of later periods.

A monk asked Zen Master Tung-shan, "What is Buddha?"
Tung-shan said, "Three pounds of flax."[1]

That's the whole case. There is a poem after the case, written by
Zen Master Wu-men (Mumon; Mu Mun):

Bursts out, "Three pounds of flax!"
Intimate speech, intimate mind.
One who speaks of right and wrong.
Is a person of right and wrong.[2]

Wu-men also writes:

Old Tozan [Tung-shan] studied a bit of clam-Zen, and
opening the shell a little, revealed his liver and intestines.
Though it may be so, tell me, where do you see Tozan?[3]

Tung-shan (Tozan; Dong Sahn) was born in 910 and lived to about
990. Originally he practiced and studied in the northwest of China,
but little by little he traveled down through China and finally came to
Yun-men's (Ummon; Un Mun) monastery in Canton Province, in the
southeast. That was a very long journey—one he made on foot, stop-
ping to practice at various temples and monasteries along the way.

Not much more is known about Tung-shan's life, except for an
interchange between him and Zen Master Yun-men when they first
met. He had traveled thousands and thousands of miles to meet Yun-
men. Yun-men asked, "Where have you been recently?" Or, "Just
now, where are you coming from?" He is asking what appears to be an
ordinary, everyday question. But at the same time he is saying, Do you
understand your true being, before name, before form, before speech,
and before words? That is where you are coming from, moment by
moment by moment. Can you reveal that to me just now?

But Tung-shan does not quite get it. So he says, "At Sah Do,
Master."

"Where did you stay last summer?"

"At Bo Ja Temple in Hoe Nam."

Yun-men again asked, "When did you leave there?"

"On the twenty-fifth day of August," answered Tung-shan.

Suddenly Yun-men changed tactics and exclaimed, "I give you sixty blows with a stick!"

Tung-shan was taken aback and retired. But he was mentally agitated and sat up all night wondering, Where is my mistake? I answered all of his questions, but he said at the end, "I give you sixty blows with a stick." That means, You good-for-nothing!

The next morning, in deep perplexity, Tung-shan returned for a second interview. He said, "Yesterday, you gave me sixty blows with a stick. I don't know where my mistake is." Yun-men said, "You rice bag! Why have you been prowling around Kang Soe and Hoe Nam?" At that—*ptchh*—Tung-shan had an enlightenment experience.[4] That is the story of their first meeting.

Yun-men was one of the most famous Zen masters in China. The Yun-men school of Zen lasted for several generations after his death, and Tung-shan was his immediate successor.

Yun-men's teaching style was famous for a couple of tactics he used when answering students' questions. One, based on the statement, "One phrase reveals three meanings," was to respond to a question with a terse answer like, "Three pounds of flax." From a logical standpoint, it would appear as if the answer had nothing to do with the question. But it was said that this kind of answer simultaneously expressed or revealed three meanings; these are called "covers heaven and earth," "cuts off all streams," and "goes along with the waves and currents."

"Covers heaven and earth" means it reveals something wide and universal. It suggests a don't-know style of teaching. You can observe it in a story about Bodhidharma (Daruma; Dalma), the first Zen patriarch, who came from India to China. When asked by the emperor of Liang, "What is the highest meaning of the holy truths?" Bodhidharma responded, "No holiness is clear like space." The emperor was taken aback and said, "Who is facing me?" Bodhidharma responded, "Don't know."[5] This "don't know" reveals something quite wide and universal. What we all know is narrow and small, but what we don't know is open and wide.

When we are thinking, we are forming our own small view of ourselves and the world. That means that each one of us has a different self-view and world-view. But at the moment that we cut off all thinking and just return to this don't-know mind, our small egocentric view falls away, and we contact the universal perspective: covering heaven and earth.

If the teacher's response stops a person's thinking mind, stops their conceptualizing mind, stops the holding or forming of any kind of opinion, it cuts off all streams.

Finally, the answer—even though it does not appear to fit logically with the question—is said to go along somehow with the person's stream of consciousness, exactly fitting what is needed at that moment, like a lid fits exactly to a box, or a hand fits exactly in a glove. In other words, it goes along with the waves and currents.

The other tactic for which he is renowned is called Yun-men's one-word Zen (or Gate). When a monk, for instance, asked Yun-men, "What is Zen?" Yun-men replied, "Kwan!" *Kwan* literally refers to a gate or barrier on a frontier pass. It is like the checkpoint between one territory and another or between two countries. But more important than the meaning is just that one sound. What is Zen, Kwan! If you look at the answer, checkpoint, in terms of what is Zen you can see that something is connoted or denoted there, something cognitive is embedded. Yun-men, as he spontaneously gave that response, could be compared to someone who writes a poem intuitively, or who composes music or paints a picture intuitively.

On another occasion, a monk asked Yun-men, "What is the straight way to Yun-men Mountain?" Now, Yun-men's temple was at the foot of the Gate of the Clouds Mountain in southern China, and in Chinese the name of the mountain is Yun-men, Cloud Gate. But the monk was not really asking about the mountain. *Mountain* also means not-moving mind, completely steady, original mind. So when the monk asked, "What is the straight way to Yun-men Mountain?" Yun-men answered, "Ch'in!" which means intimacy or closeness. Then the monk asked Yun-men, "What is the sword of Yun-men?" and Yun-men replied, "Tsu," which means ancestor.

Once Yun-men was asked, "What kind of speech goes beyond buddhas and patriarchs?" Yun-men replied, "Ricecake." That is a perfect one-word poem.

Here is an example of Tung-shan's one-word Zen that connects directly with the don't-know tradition:

A monk asked Tung-shan, "What is the sword of
 Tung-shan?"
Tung-shan said, "Why?"
The monk said, "I want to know."
Tung-shan said, "Blasphemy!"[6]

At the moment Tung-shan said "Why?" he showed the monk his sword. His why was like Yun-men's ricecake. It cut off all thinking, leaving only *Ohhhhhh!!* But the monk did not understand that he already had his answer and replied, "I want to know." That is the primary Zen mistake: I want to know something. Tung-shan responded, "Blasphemy!"

That is the background of this style. Although we refer to it as Yun-men's one-word Zen, he did not originate it. Stories about Zen Master Chao-chou (Joshu; Joju), from about sixty years earlier, show him giving similarly terse answers. When a monk asked him, "Does a dog have the buddha nature?" Chao-chou answered, "Mu," which literally means no. On another occasion, a monk asked Chao-chou, "Why did the first patriarch, Bodhidharma, come to China?" and he responded, "The cypress tree in the garden." That is the same style. "Cypress tree in the garden" does not appear to have anything to do with why Bodhidharma went to China. But on a deeper level, it connects with the question and the questioner very intimately.

Let us return to the case, where the monk asked Tung-shan, "What is Buddha?" and he replied, "Three pounds of flax." Many commentators say that perhaps Tung-shan was weighing flax when he was asked the question. In China and Korea, flax and hemp are used to make linen-like fabrics that the monks use for their summer robes. But more important than whether he was weighing flax is the quality of Tung-shan's response, which comes forth spontaneously. It is direct, it is vital; he projects his whole being with this one word. In Chinese, "three pounds of flax" is represented by one sound, one character.

In this style, once a question is asked, the response shoots back immediately, almost like an echo: question–response; question–response. That is sometimes referred to as mirror-mind Zen or great mirror wisdom, because just like a mirror, which does not hold any color of its own, it immediately reflects back whatever comes in front of it. This style of answer does not color anything with subjective projections of any kind.

If you look at the monk's question, it asks *what* is Buddha, not *who* is Buddha. It is not asking about some particular person; it is asking about a principle, a universal principle called buddha. Literally, *buddha* comes from a Sanskrit root that has the connotation of "awake" or "to wake up." Thus, What is Buddha? means, What is this awake state that is present in each and every thing, and in each and every moment? Please show it to me. Tung-shan responds, "Three pounds of flax!"

That question—What is buddha?—is common in Zen stories. In Wu-men's collection of kong-ans, it appears several times. For example: A monk asked Zen Master Ma-tsu (Baso; Ma-Jo), "What is buddha?" Ma-tsu responded, "Mind is buddha; buddha is mind." That answer is not bad, although it is a little conceptual. It can lead to the thought that I have mind, he has mind, she has mind, everybody has mind; so if I want to find buddha, I have to look into my own mind. The problem is, where you started out with one concept, buddha, now you have a second concept, mind. If you stay with that for a while, you begin to wonder, Well mind is buddha, but what is this mind? If you come to that level, where you have a special question—What is this mind?—then you reach cuts-off-all-streams point again.

On another day when a monk asked, "What is buddha?" Zen Master Ma-tsu gave a different answer: "No mind, no buddha." In Japanese and Korean, the word for no is *mu*. Thus in Korean, "no mind" is *mu shim,* and "no buddha" is *mu bul.*

Sometimes when someone becomes a monk or nun in these countries, they are given the Buddhist name Mu Shim or Mu Bul—No Mind or No Buddha. "No mind, no buddha" means no inside, no outside; no subject, no object; no good, no bad; no relative versus absolute; and ultimately no mu—no no. That is important: Do not get too attached to mu, to no.

Once when a monk asked Yun-men, "What is buddha?" he replied, "Dry shit-stick." Yun-men, just like Tung-shan, revealed himself completely through "dry shit-stick." It is secondary whether or not he was just coming from the outhouse, where twigs were used in lieu of toilet paper. When a monk named Hui-ch'ao (Echo; Hae Cho) asked Zen Master Fa-yen (Hogen; Peop An), "What is buddha," Fa-yen said, "You are Hui-ch'ao."

Let's take another look at Tung-shan's answer, "Three pounds of flax." There is something absolute about that three pounds of flax. A teacher in ancient times said, "Just this live three pounds; just this dead three pounds; just this adverse three pounds; just this favorable three pounds. Wherever you may go, it is the same amount. How vast is this three pounds!"[7] Immeasurable! The meaning transcends buddhas and demons, life and death, time and space.

A Zen poem says:

"What is Buddha?"
"Three pounds of flax," he answers.
Not increasing or decreasing;
Just as it is![8]

This practice of transcending time and space, inside and outside, subject and object, good and bad with a phrase like "three pounds of flax" is sometimes called *huat'ou* practice in Chinese, or *hwadu* in Korean Zen. Both literally mean "word head"—head of speech, ante-word, the moment before words and speech, before names and forms appear.

Usually the practice of hwadu involves a question of some kind. There are two main styles: The first is a question that is directly about our own nature, some fundamental, existential question, such as, When you are born, where do you come from? When you die, where will you go? No one knows. If you hold that in your mind, you come to a point where everything is cut off. That moment is before speech and words; you cannot compare it to anything else, so it is not relative.

Here is another example of the same style: What is your original face, before your parents were born? Everyone understands that their face comes from their parents, but what is your original face, before your parents were even born? Those are variants of What am I? or Who am I? or What is this? What is mind?

That is one style of hwadu. If you use a question like, What am I? it seems very slippery. You feel as if you cannot get any focus. And if you want focus, you will become quite frustrated, even if you repeat the word *I* to yourself over and over: "I . . . I . . . I . . . I." Behind the word *I* lies the question, What does *I* refer to? After a while, you can't hold on to anything, because you can't really make an object out of yourself. If you try to hold on to something and do not accept the frustration of it as part of the process, then it becomes problematic.

The second style of hwadu is similar to the one-word answers. The Zen master might say to a student, "The monk asked Tung-shan, What is Buddha? Tung-shan replied, Three pounds of flax. What was his meaning?" Or, "What was his intent?" Or, "What was his mind?" Or, "Why did he say, Three pounds of flax?" Then you think, Three pounds of flax. Why did he say that? Three pounds of flax. Why? You are left with the same don't-know.

After a while, if you keep holding "three pounds of flax" in your mind, the *why* drops off; then three pounds of flax is don't-know, and don't-know is three pounds of flax. The mind stops. All streams are cut off; no increasing, no decreasing; neither favorable nor unfavorable, it remains constant no matter what. Just three pounds.

Now, look at Wu-men's comment again: "Old Tung-shan studied a bit of clam-Zen, and opening the shell a little, revealed his liver and intestines. Though it may be so, tell me, where do you see Tung-shan?" That is an interesting expression, clam-Zen. It means that when he opened his mouth and exclaimed, "Three pounds of flax," it was as if he were showing his complete substance all at once. If a clam opens, you see everything; there is nothing held back; it is completely exposed. Three pounds of flax! There are his liver and intestines, his gall bladder. The whole substance of him, undivided, appears. *Tuumm!* Three pounds of flax.

We have an expression in English, "closed like a clam." Or sometimes we say somebody "clammed up." It is a complaint you hear more from women about men. It usually goes: I tried to get him to talk about himself, I tried to get him to say what was on his mind, I tried to get him to express his feelings, but he just closed up like a clam.

Zen teaching is always encouraging us to let go, to open, to present ourselves, to expose ourselves, to disclose ourselves. When Hui-chung (Chu Kokushi; Hae Chung) asked Zen Master Ma-tsu, "What is essential in Buddhism?" Ma-tsu said, "Just to let go of yourself and your life." To let go of yourself and your life does not mean to commit suicide. It means that we all make this thing that we call "my life," as if it were something quite special and precious. In making my life, we miss the fundamental fact that each of our individual lives is continuously and always rooted in the universal life of this world and the cosmos. So Ma-tsu replied to "What is essential in Buddhism?" with "Just to let go of yourself"—open, release, and let go of *your* life.

Of course, shells can sometimes be useful. If you are a clam, for example, and you want to keep out sand and irritants, it is helpful to be able to close up. But sometimes we act as if things are irritants when in fact they are really requests, asking us to become more fully alive. And in mistaking these requests for irritants, we close off. Our shell—which might have a useful function at times—becomes a jail cell.

I think there are two aspects of this disclose-yourself Zen practice. One is to disclose yourself in front of yourself; let yourself see your guts and your intestines—the whole business. That is why, for example, when we sit meditation the instructions are always, Don't push anything away. Just be with each thing, become one with every thing as it unfolds, but do not cling to it, do not hold it. Let it come and let it go, just as a mirror lets red and white come and go. Disclose yourself to yourself.

The second aspect is to disclose yourself to the other person. Be open; do not hold back. You see that emphasized in formal Zen training during the interview between teacher and student. Sometimes the student will come in and present an answer to a kong-an, but the teacher will say, Even if that answer were correct, it is not correct. That means you have not completely presented yourself as that answer. Or the teacher might say, I can't believe that, even if it is correct. Other times the teacher will say to the student, If only you believed that! This is an encouragement to disclose yourself, to expose yourself, to reveal yourself, and to not hold back.

Notes

1. See Seung Sahn, trans., *The Mu Mun Kwan* (Cumberland, RI: Kwan Um School of Zen, 1983), 22.
2. Ibid.
3. Zenkei Shibayama, *The Gateless Barrier* (Boston: Shambhala, 2000), 134.
4. See Seung Sahn, *Mu Mun Kwan*, 18.
5. Seung Sahn, trans., *The Blue Cliff Record* (Cumberland, RI: Kwan Um School of Zen, 1983), 1.
6. See Chang Chung-yuan, trans., *Original Teachings of Ch'an Buddhism* (New York: Grove Press, 1995), 299.
7. Shibayama, 136.
8. Ibid.

CHAPTER 15

Hsuan-sha's Three Kinds of Sick People

Can you see clearly?

Do you hear clearly?

Can you say something to the point?

Haahh!!

Two eyes, two ears, one mouth. Already complete.

Don't make a problem.

Zen Master Hsueh-feng (Seppo; Seol Bong) had two successors, from whom two of the five schools of Zen arose. They were Yun-men (Ummon; Un Mun) and Hsuan-sha (Gensha; Hyeon Sa). (We focused on Yun-men in chapters 13 and 14.) Hsuan-sha's was the penultimate Zen school in China, which flourished widely for several generations. The school from Hsuan-sha's dharma grandson, Fa-yen (Hogen; Peop An) was the last school to emerge, although in some of the old chronicles Fa-yen's school is referred to as the Hsuan-sha school. So originally people associated the teaching with Hsuan-sha. And it is said that Hsuan-sha had absorbed Hsueh-feng's teachings so well that he presented them even better than his teacher. So perhaps the last school should be called Hsueh-feng's school.

In any case, Hsuan-sha grew up illiterate. When young, he liked to go fishing, so he became a fisherman and supported himself that way until he was thirty years old.

Then he suddenly got an urge to become a monk, so he went to Zen Master Ling-hsun and took novice precepts. In the monastery, Hsuan-sha acted as if Hsueh-feng were his teacher, even though Ling-hsun was also Hsueh-feng's first teacher. Hsuan-sha's practice style was rather ascetic, and this made Hsueh-feng refer to Hsuan-sha as Ascetic Pei, because his dharma name was Shih Pei.

On one occasion, Hsueh-feng asked him, "Which one is the true Ascetic Pei?" To which Hsuan-sha replied, "I would never dare to deceive anyone."

When Hsueh-feng started his own teaching school, Hsuan-sha went with him to a place called Elephant Bone Mountain and helped him build a monastery there. At a certain point, Hsueh-feng said to Hsuan-sha, "Why don't you go travel around and call on other Zen teachers?" Hsuan-sha set out on his journey. On his way, he stumbled, stubbing his toe severely. At that moment, he was awakened. He exclaimed, "Bodhidharma never came to China. The Second Patriarch never got transmission." After Hsueh-feng approved his experience and gave him transmission, Hsuan-sha began to teach on his own.

One day he mounted the rostrum and was about to start his dharma talk when he suddenly heard a swallow chirping outside the dharma room. He remained silent for some time, just listening. Then he said to the assembly, "What a profound discourse on reality and a clear exposition of the dharma!" He then got down from the rostrum and returned to his room.

This short anecdote relates to case 88 in *The Blue Cliff Record*, titled "Hsuan-sha's Three Kinds of Sick People." The kong-an has two paragraphs. The first paragraph says:

> Hsuan-sha, teaching his assembly, said, "The old adepts everywhere all speak of relating to things for all people. If they unexpectedly encountered three kinds of sick people, how would they relate to them? With a blind

person, they could pick up the gavel or raise the whisk, but he wouldn't see it. With a deaf person, he wouldn't understand the samadhi of words. With a mute person, if they had him speak, he wouldn't be able to speak. But how would they relate to such people? If they couldn't relate to these people, then the Buddha Dharma has no miraculous effect."[1]

It is curious that he refers to people who are blind and deaf and mute not as having an affliction or handicap but as sick people. That is a hint about something in the kong-an, because we would not ordinarily refer to those conditions as sicknesses.

This paragraph makes three important points.

First he says, "The old adepts [the old Zen masters, the old teachers] everywhere all speak of relating to things for all people." Another translation says "guiding and aiding living beings."[2] A third says, "saving things and delivering mankind."[3] But however you translate it, the focus is on all beings. It is talking about cultivating the spirit of altruism in practice—practice not just being for myself but for all beings.

The second point is, What is the meaning of blind, deaf, and mute?

And the third point lies in the last sentence: "If they couldn't relate to these people, then the Buddha Dharma has no miraculous effect."

So, what is the miraculous effect of the buddha dharma?

Layman P'ang said that his miraculous effect of practice was to be found in chopping wood and hauling water. It is in recognizing that when hungry, you eat, and when tired, you sleep. This is the great Zen miracle.

The first point, "for all beings," alludes to the direction of practice. In Mahayana Buddhism, that is called the bodhisattva path. One of the main practices of this path is the six paramitas. The first is dana paramita. *Dana* is sometimes translated as "generosity" or "giving," and *paramita* has the connotation of crossing over and transcending. You could translate *dana paramita* as "transcends opposites generosity"—a generosity that transcends opposites. *Dana* also has the connotation of giving and nonattachment, of warmth and openness. If you manifest the spirit of openness and warmth, then there is already giving and nonclinging. And in that openness and warmth and nonclinging, generosity emerges. That is the meaning of "for all beings."

It is said that the Bodhisattva of Compassion, Avalokiteshvara, is always giving the gift of fearlessness. The Heart Sutra relates that "Avalokiteshvara perceives that all five skandhas are empty and is saved from all suffering and distress." This perception leads to the elimination of fear. If you perceive that the notion of self-sufficiency is nothing more than an empty concept, and that what is really true is our interconnectedness, then the need to establish rigid boundaries drops away, and you are not afraid of losing anything. Thus the perception of interconnectedness leads to fearlessness—there is no need for me to be guarding myself from you.

A story about Chao-chou (Joshu; Joju) represents his practice of "for all beings." A monk asked Chao-chou, "For a long time, I've heard of the stone bridge of Chao-chou [the name of the town where Chao-chou was Zen master], but now that I've come here, I just see a simple log bridge."

This is a bit of Zen double-talk, because he is not really talking about a bridge in the town of Chao-chou. He is talking about Chao-chou the Zen teacher and saying, "For a long time I've heard about the great Zen master Chao-chou. All over China I've heard about him. But now that I have made the long journey to come here and meet you face-to-face, you don't look so marvelous, like a great stone bridge. You look simple and ordinary." Chao-chou was plain. He mended his robe over and over and sat on a stool that had one broken leg. He was, however, quite formidable in his ordinariness. In answer to the monk, he said, "You just see the log bridge; you don't see the stone bridge." In other words, it's in the eye of the beholder. The monk asked, "What is the stone bridge?" Chao-chan said, "Asses cross, horses cross."[4] He didn't even say, "Asses cross over it, horses cross over it." Just, "Asses cross, horses cross."

The stability of this great stone bridge is to be found in asses crossing, horses crossing. That means that in opening up and letting all beings move freely, there is the stability of a great stone bridge.

This is very much the spirit of Zen meditation: to be able to just open to what is and let things come and go freely. In that allowance—letting things be as they are—is already the spirit of generosity and giving and warmth and openness. So we practice over and over again, day in, day out, to reconnect with that generosity in many different forms, for all beings.

Then Hsuan-sha talks about three kinds of sickness: deafness, blindness, and muteness.

Sometimes Zen language is concrete and metaphorical at the same time. For example, once a thief came to the hut of a Zen master who was living as a hermit. The master said, "Oh, you want my money? You can take my money. Please take my robe, too, and take all these things on the wall." He gave the thief everything he had, and the thief left. The master was sitting there completely naked, looking out the window at the moon. He said, "I wish I could have given him this beautiful moon, as well."

Now, to give the beautiful moon, one has to give the mind that can perceive the beautiful moon. If someone is entrenched in an attitude of deprivation, then open mind is unavailable. Often in Zen poetry the moon is used as a representation of original mind—round and full and brightly luminous. So the master is also saying, I wish I could give him this simple experience of just sitting and looking at the moon. I wish I could transmit this mind to him.

In the kong-an are the terms *deaf*, *blind*, and *mute*. Those terms have three different meanings. First, there is the basic deafness, blindness, and muteness connected with the infirmity of ignorance. If you are ignoring what is truly clear and present, then you do not see. And if you are holding on to your own ignorance and limiting view, you do not hear the ever-present teaching that is going on in the car horns and the bird song or in an argument with your friend. And if you are not in touch with your simple, original being, then your manifestation through speech is not clear, direct, and straightforward. That is one form of blindness, deafness, and muteness.

The second meaning of deaf, blind, and mute refers to certain kinds of deep meditation that are focused on developing a profound sense of inner quiet.

A friend of mine recently went to a health spa where there was a flotation tank. He said it was like a bathtub in a darkened, soundproof room. There was so much salt in the water that he was buoyant to the point of virtual weightlessness.

This friend is someone I know from my years of yoga training. His relationship to meditation is much more from that school than from Zen meditation. He said to me, "When I sit and meditate, my body is always a little bit problematic. I never quite get rid of this or that tension and just let go and transcend my body sense." But, he said, "In the flotation tank, I was able to completely let go, and the body was not problematic at all. I was able to really go deep inside and become very, very quiet, with no distractions."

In the yoga view of meditation, there is the notion of withdrawing the senses from the objects of the senses, so transcendence is to withdraw from sound and sight and external touch, to go beyond those things into a state of deep inner quiet. He described his experience in the tank as facilitating that. That would be the second form of deaf, blind, and mute. You don't see anything, you don't hear anything, you don't even think anything; there's no chatter. In meditation traditions, that is sometimes called *samadhi*.

From the Zen perspective, if that experience were to come in your meditation practice spontaneously, you would just welcome it and be there. And if it passed away, it would pass away. But if you began to cling to that kind of experience, and wanted that kind of inner quiet, and directed yourself toward cultivating that as the sole object of your practice, then Zen teaching would call that "falling down in emptiness." At that point, you would have lost your eyes, your ears, your nose, your tongue, your body. You would have lost everything. You would be in the Cave of Emptiness without being able to get out.

Zen transcendence is a little different from that. Zen transcendence says, Hit the world of opposites and become one. In that experience, the eyes, the object of sight, and the process of seeing all interfuse and become one. At that moment, we completely attain the whiteness of the wall and the brownness of the floor—we completely fall into this world. This experience is sometimes paradoxically referred to as becoming completely blind, completely deaf. There is no separating of eyes from what is seen, of ears from what is heard. It is just white! Just like that.

One commentary on this first half of the kong-an says: Truly blind, deaf, or mute. This is guiding and aiding living beings. One does not have to be blind not to see. One does not have to be deaf not to hear. Who hasn't heard yet? One doesn't have to be mute to be unable to speak. Who hasn't spoken yet?[5]

Hsuan-sha often used the teaching device of the three sicknesses when he gave a dharma talk. He would say, "You better not make your understanding in terms of blind, deaf, and mute."[6] That means he is not talking about psychic healing, as if a great Zen adept should be able to cure the infirmities of blindness, deafness, and muteness.

Once a monk came forward in the assembly and said to Hsuan-sha, "Master, may I present you with a theory of the three sicknesses?" Hsuan-sha said, "Yes, of course." The monk immediately said, "Master, I bid you farewell," and walked away. Hsuan-sha said, "Wrong! That's not it."[7]

Now let's consider the second part of case 88. This teaching of Hsuan-sa's became well known. At one time a monk went to Hsuan-sa's dharma brother, Yun-men, and asked for instruction about it. Yun-men said, "Bow." The monk bowed and rose. Yun-men poked at him with his staff. The monk drew back. Yun-men said, "You're not blind."

Now, one important question is, What is the you that is not blind? A comment says, "Truly blind. Better not say this monk is blind. The Bodhisattva of Compassion has come."[8]

An old teacher said, "His eyes see forms as though blind, and his ears hear sounds as though deaf."[9] A poem on this point says:

Though it fills his eyes, he doesn't see form;
Though it fills his ears, he doesn't hear sound—

> Manjushri is always covering his eyes,
> Avalokiteshvara blocks his ears.[10]

Manjushri, the Bodhisattva of Wisdom, who has the wisdom eye, the clear-seeing eye, is covering his eyes. Avalokiteshvara, the Bodhisattva of Compassion, who has realized true being through hearing, is blocking his ears.

To continue with the story: Yun-men said, "You're not blind." Then Yun-men called him closer; when the monk approached, Yun-men said, "You're not deaf." Next Yun-men said, "Do you understand?" The monk said, "I don't understand."

Now the monk is getting somewhere. That "I don't understand" is quite potent. At that moment, Yun-men has taken away all his ideas, all his concepts. The monk thought there was something to learn about Hsuan-sha's teaching of the three sicknesses. But at this point he absolutely doesn't understand.

Then Yun-men said, "You're not mute." At that, the monk attained.

What did he get? At the moment of, "I don't understand" and "You're not mute," the monk gets *"Oh!"* At that moment, he sees with his whole being, he hears with his whole being, he speaks with his whole being. When he opens his mouth and completely and honestly proclaims, "I don't understand"—*ptchh!* There he is. That is the miraculous effect of the Zen tradition.

Ti-ts'ang (Rakan; Nan Ha), one of Hsuan-sha's successors, said to Fa-yen, his student, "What is the meaning of your pilgrimage?" Fa-yen said, "I don't know." Ti-ts'ang said, "Don't know is most intimate. Not knowing is closest to it." That means, at the moment of don't-know you perceive with your whole being. There are no eyes, no ears, no nose, no tongue, no body, no mind—one's whole being hears, sees, and opens the mouth and speaks. There is no sense of separation. At that point, one realizes that eyes, ears, and mouth are fundamentally and originally already illuminated, already shining brightly. Just seeing is buddha nature. It's all of one piece. That is Zen transcendence. The transcendent matter is sometimes called true blindness.

After the case is a poem. The first part of the poem alludes to some old Chinese masters of legendary times who were said to possess mystic sight and mystic hearing. But the poet says, after referring to them,

> How can this compare to sitting alone beneath an empty
> window?
> The leaves fall, the flowers bloom—each in its own time.[11]

Leaves fall; it's autumn. Flowers bloom; it's spring. Seeing and not seeing; hearing and not hearing. How are they different?

Haahh!!

The wall is white; the floor is brown.

Notes

1. Seung Sahn, trans., *The Blue Cliff Record* (Cumberland, RI: Kwan Um School of Zen, 1983), 67.
2. Thomas Cleary and J. C. Cleary, trans., *The Blue Cliff Record* (Boston: Shambhala, 1992), 482.
3. Katsuki Sekida, trans., *Two Zen Classics: Mumonkan and Hekiganroku* (New York: Weatherhill, 1977), 372.
4. Seung Sahn, 43.
5. See Cleary and Cleary, 483.
6. Ibid., 485.
7. See ibid., 484.
8. See ibid., 483.
9. Ibid., 485.
10. Ibid.
11. Ibid., 486.

CHAPTER 16

You Are Hui-ch'ao

If you attain the zero point, you become free.

If you attach to zero, you become trapped.

Going past those two, you manifest great action.

But what is manifesting great action?

Haahh!!

If you want to ride the lion, then be prepared to enter the lion's den.

Case 7 in *The Blue Cliff Record* cites a short interchange between Zen Master Fa-yen (Hogen; Poep An) and the monk named Hui-ch'ao (Echo; Hae Cho).

A monk named Hui Ch'ao asked Fa Yen, "Hui Ch'ao asked the Master, What is Buddha?"
    Fa Yen said, "You are Hui Ch'ao."[1]

This could be interpreted as: Master, my name is Hui-ch'ao, please tell me, what is Buddha? Fay-yen said, "You are Hui-ch'ao." That is like, "What is Buddha?" "You are Ken." Or, "You are Sarah, and you are Alan."

At a jazz concert I went to recently, the leader of the group said, "I want to dedicate this tune to the great master Duke Ellington." Duke Ellington, of course, followed his own way all the time. "And," the leader added, "the title is 'Be Yourself.'" Then he paused for a moment and said, "You might as well be. Who else could you be?" Similarly, Shakespeare says in Sonnet 84, "that you alone are you." From a Zen standpoint, the leader was stating a notion about freedom: Be yourself. Who else do you think you could actually be? After playing the "fitting game" for eons after eons, we all become tired and come back to a recognition that there is no one else to be but who we are. And in the acceptance of that no choice or one choice or only one way, we find a certain kind of freedom. Not freedom in the sense of do whatever you please, but freedom in owning the real possibility of what is. Zen Master Fa-yen's teaching was very much connected with that.

When Fa-yen was a student, he traveled around with two other monks, going from one Zen master, one Zen community, to another. It was a tradition at that time in China, and those who participated were called cloud and water monks—suggesting that they were totally free, just drifting from one place to another, like clouds floating in the sky or water flowing in a stream. In a certain sense, that was a practice of cultivating nonattachment by not being in any one place for very long.

But when Fa-yen and his traveling companions arrived at the monastery of Ti-ts'ang (Rakan; Nan Ha), bad weather forced them stay there. Ti-ts'ang asked Fa-yen, "What is the meaning of your traveling around?" Fa-yen had no immediate answer and felt momentarily stuck. Then he just said, "Don't know." Zen Master Ti-ts'ang said, "Not knowing is closest to it." When Fa-yen heard that, he had an opening and decided to remain with Ti-ts'ang to make his realization more firm and certain.

Later, when he decided to move on, he went to tell the master about his decision. Ti-ts'ang said, "You always say that the whole world is mind only, and that the myriad phenomena are all just consciousness. Those rocks over there in the garden, are they inside your mind or outside your mind?" Fa-yen replied, "Inside my mind. How could anything be outside?" In response Ti-ts'ang said, "What use does a

Zen traveler have to put a rock inside his head?" Again Fa-yen was stuck. He put down his bag and decided to stay a while longer.

Let's look at that question: What need does a Zen student, a Zen traveler, have to put a rock inside his head? Of course, we all have put so many things in our heads that it's a wonder we can retain an upright posture.

You can take that question two ways. First as a challenge: Why are you carrying that with you? The challenge cuts off thinking, and in that instant you drop it; it is gone, or stuckness is experienced. But simultaneously you can look at the question as an invitation to inquire sincerely: Yes, what need do I have to be carrying this stuff in my head? What do I imagine it is doing for me?

Some time ago, I was talking to a friend whose father is about ninety years old. My friend said, "My father is very old, and I know I should see him more frequently than I do. But I don't want to. But I obsess about my father all the time." I asked him, "What does that do for you?" He said, "I guess I make myself feel guilty."

My friend feels he should see his father more frequently, but he is not going physically to see him. Instead, he carries his father around with him in his own internal make-believe world. And by doing that he accomplishes seeing his father. Of course, a picture of a sandwich does not fill your stomach, so there is a limitation to that approach.

After Zen Master Ti-ts'ang asked Fa-yen, "What need does a Zen traveler have to put a rock inside his head?" Fa-yen put down his bag and decided to stay again. He would go to Ti-ts'ang every day, presenting his view, and Ti-ts'ang would just say, "The buddha dharma is not like that" and dismiss him. This went on for about a month. Fa-yen would go out and come back the next day with some other presentation. And Ti-ts'ang would say, "No, the buddha dharma is not like that either."

Finally Fa-yen came one day and said, "All my words and ideas are completely exhausted." To which Ti-ts'ang responded, "Yes, that mind is the rocks and the great earth and the blue sky and the trees and the myriad phenomena in their completeness." At that moment, Fa-yen's mind opened and became one with all that.

So Fa-yen understood through his own training the practice of repeatedly attaining something and having it taken away. Finally, that which had been partially realized earlier became complete.

Later, when he was teaching, he often made use of a similar procedure. Once a monk from another temple was staying in Fa-yen's assembly and had yet to approach Fa-yen for instruction. Fa-yen asked him, "Why have you never entered my room privately?" In other words, How come you never come for private instruction, for a Zen interview? The monk replied, "Oh, didn't you know, master? When I was with the previous assembly, I had an awakening there." Meaning, I don't need to come to your room because I already understand. Then Fa-yen said, "Please present it to me." The monk said, "I asked the teacher, 'What is buddha?' And the teacher said, 'The fire god comes seeking fire.'" Fa-yen looked at him and said, "Well, those are wonderful words. But I think you have misunderstood. Can you say some more about it?" The monk said, "The fire god is already in the province of fire, and yet he comes seeking fire. Likewise, I am already buddha, but I came asking about buddha." Fa-yen observed, "It's just as I thought. You have completely misunderstood."[2]

The monk became angry but contained himself out of respect and to observe the proper decorum. However, he left the monastery, crossed the river, and began to walk away on the road.

Fa-yen said to the assembly, "If this monk comes back, he can be saved. If not, he can't." That is an important point for all of us. If you can return to beginner's mind over and over again, manifesting the mind of openness, then that attitude is your salvation. But if you cannot turn back to that, regardless of what you have experienced or known or accomplished, then you are trapped. Your ego begins to creep in, and that is a big problem. In our practice, we have to repeatedly remind ourselves of that point. Over and over again, come back to the attitude of a beginner. Because even if you know something, you don't know it fully. That is why it is said that even the Buddha is still practicing.

Meanwhile, the monk out on the road thought to himself, Master Fa-yen is the teacher of five hundred people; why would he deceive me? A little opening, a little space appeared in the monk's conscious-ness, and he decided, I'll go back and see. So he went back and pre-sented himself before Fa-yen, who said to him, "Just ask me, and I'll set the matter straight for you." The monk said, "What is buddha?" And Fa-yen replied, "The fire god comes seeking fire." Boom! The monk got it.

On another occasion, an elder monk from another assembly came to Fa-yen's temple. Fa-yen quoted an old discourse that had to do with the phrase "one unique body manifesting amidst the myriad phenomena." Then he looked at the elder monk and said, "What is the unique body amidst the myriad phenomena?" The elder held up the Zen stick. Fa-yen said, "How can you understand it that way?" The elder replied, "What is the venerable teacher's view on the mat-ter?" In response Fa-yen said, "What is it that you call the myriad phenomena?" The elder said, "The ancients did not eliminate the myriad phenomena."

The monk thought that the purpose of Fa-yen's response was to negate everything. It's similar to saying all individual existences are just like clouds in the sky; their forms and existences are all fleeting and empty. Everything really returns to nothing. That's how the monk understood Fa-yen's response, "What is it actually that you call the myriad phenomena?" But again, as a practice direction, you can look at that question in another way, just as an intention or an invitation to be open. What is it actually that we are calling Ken, Sarah, and Alan? What is this? "The ancients never eliminated the myriad phenomena" means that the Zen way is not to make everything into one big zero. There is no need to take away the myriad phenomena, no need to eliminate the unique differences between everybody and everything. That is not the Zen way. The Zen way is to see the truth amidst all these things.

Fa-yen responded to the monk again, "One unique body amidst the myriad phenomena. What has eliminating or not eliminating got to do with it?" Boom! The monk grasped it experientially.

What has eliminating or not eliminating got to do with it? What has making better or worse got to do with the essential matter? What has evaluating it in any particular way got to do with it? Hui-ch'ao asked, "What is buddha?" And Fa-yen said, "You are Hui-ch'ao." No good, no bad, no eliminating, no not eliminating. Just, you are you. When you become you, then Zen becomes Zen, and buddha becomes buddha.

It is important to make an effort to be Hui-ch'ao if you are Hui-ch'ao. Who else could you be?

Notes

1. Seung Sahn, trans., *The Blue Cliff Record* (Cumberland, RI: Kwan Um School of Zen, 1983), 7.
2. See Chang Chung-yuan, trans., *Original Teachings of Ch'an Buddhism* (New York: Grove Press, 1995), 231.

CHAPTER 17

Hsiang-lin's Meaning of the Coming from the West

. . . .

Can you say that this matter of Zen is long or short?

When you get to the zero point, are all meanings completely exhausted or are all meanings completely enlivened?

At this point, is there coming and going, or not?

What can you say about these three matters?

Haahh!!

Just now reading black marks on white paper.

. . . .

Case 17 in *The Blue Cliff Record*, "Hsiang-lin's Meaning of the Coming from the West," is just two sentences long:

A monk asked Hsiang-lin, "What is the meaning of the Patriarch's [Bodhidharma] coming from the West?"

Hsiang-lin said, "Sitting for a long time becomes wearisome."[1]

I consider Hsiang-lin (Kyorin; Hyang Rim) to be one of the great heroes in the Zen tradition, even though not much is known about him. Born in 908, he lived until 987. He grew up in Szechuan Province in the west-central part of China. In his late teens—by then probably already a monk—he heard about the many famous Zen masters living in the south of China. Setting off on foot, he gradually made his way to Canton Province in southeast China, a journey of over a thousand miles. He arrived at the temple of Yun-men (Ummon; Un Mun) and studied with the Zen master while serving as his attendant for eighteen or twenty years. After Yun-men gave him permission to teach, he returned to Szechuan Province and became the teacher at Hsiang-lin Monastery (from whence his name is derived), residing there for forty years. His story, from his training with Yun-men to his enlightenment, is both interesting and inspiring.

Although there are various versions of his story, all tell of one almost daily incident: Hsiang-lin would be taking leave of Yun-men. Then Yun-men would suddenly call out, "Attendant!" Hsiang-lin would turn around and reply, "Yes?" Yun-men would just ask, "What is it?" This went on for eighteen years. One version says that the only instruction Hsiang-lin ever received from Yun-men was this "Attendant!" "Yes?" "What is it?" It is hard to imagine that that was really the only instruction he ever received, but it makes a good story. Then, no matter what answer Hsiang-lin would give, Yun-men would discount it, saying something like, The buddha dharma is not like that.

You can imagine what that kind of response would kick up in someone. Every day, whatever you presented—even if you did not present anything—the teacher would just say, No, that's not it. Most students who come for Zen interviews know how it feels when you have worked on a kong-an for a few weeks or months but are still unable to pass it. Imagine this guy: For eighteen years, whatever he answered, he was just dismissed.

One day, however, when Yun-men asked, "What is it?" Hsiang-lin suddenly said, "Oh, I understand." Yun-men immediately replied, "Why don't you say something beyond and above just that?" The story does not tell us what Hsiang-lin said after that, but it does report that he stayed on for another three years before returning to his native province as a teacher.

One other story about Hsiang-lin's training days tells how Yun-men forbade students to write down any of his talks, responses, or teachings. Hsiang-lin, however, secretly gathered the teachings by writing them on a paper robe. Once he had recorded them, Hsiang-lin passed them on to another disciple, who organized them into the form that became the *Record of the Essential Words of Ch'an Master K'uang-chen from Mount Yun-men*. That is the reason we have so many stories about Yun-men.

Besides the present kong-an, which is the only time that Hsiang-lin's teaching appears in the main kong-an collections, we have a few other examples of his responses to students.

One student asked, "How is it when both self and object are completely forgotten?" Hsiang-lin said, "Sitting, sleeping with your eyes open." Another student asked, "How can I attain the understanding of the mind of all the buddhas?" Hsiang-lin replied, "Don't be fooled by people." On another occasion, a monk asked, "What is the meaning of Bodhidharma's coming to China?" Hsiang-lin said, "Who's the one who's walking?"

When another student asked, "What is the master's marvelous medicine?" Hsiang-lin replied, "It's not apart from the myriad flavors."

In Chinese herbal medicine, medicines are categorized by five or six tastes, such as salty, bitter, sweet, sour, and astringent. When Hsiang-lin answered that his marvelous medicine is not apart from the myriad flavors, he was referring to our experience in the world. Moment-by-moment is a multitude of flavors, a multitude of colors, a multitude of experiences. So what is the master's marvelous medicine? It is not apart from your many experiences.

Then the student asked, "How is the one who has taken it?" Hsiang-lin replied, "Why not sip some yourself and see?" That is an important point: Do not sit around talking about all this, conceptualizing and philosophizing; sip some yourself and see.

Now we come back to the case. There are two parts: First the monk's question, "What is the meaning of the Patriarch Bodhidharma's coming from the west?"

According to legend, Bodhidharma (Daruma; Dalma) took three years to journey from India to China when he was quite advanced in age. His teacher had told him, "When you go to China, don't stay long in the south, or else the dharma will die out."

Bodhidharma landed in the south of China, where he had an audience with the emperor of a small kingdom. This emperor, a patron of Buddhism, had sponsored the rebuilding of many temples as well as the ordination ceremonies of many monks and nuns. The emperor said to Bodhidharma, "I've built many temples and supported and fed many monks and nuns. What kind of merit do I get for all that?" Bodhidharma replied, "None." The emperor was surprised; the Buddhism flourishing in China at that time taught that good deeds bring merit, leading to a better rebirth. The emperor said to Bodhidharma, "Then what is the highest meaning of the Holy Truths?" Bodhidharma answered, "No holiness is clear like space." Again the emperor was surprised. He asked, "Who is this standing in front of me?" Bodhidharma responded, "Don't know" This is the first historic example in the Zen tradition of don't-know mind. But the emperor did not understand Bodhidharma's "don't know."

After that, Bodhidharma continued his journey. He crossed the Yangtze River and went to Shaolin Temple. According to the story, he sat there for nine years, facing the wall. Then one student, Hui-k'o (Eka), appeared. Bodhidharma asked him, "What do you want of me?" Hui-k'o said, "My mind is not at peace, please pacify my mind." Bodhidharma said, "Give me your mind, and I'll put it to rest for you." Hui-k'o replied, "When I look for my mind, I can't find it." Bodhidharma told Hui-k'o, "Then I've already put your mind to rest."

That is the story of Bodhidharma's coming from the west. If you look at it, Bodhidharma embodies the true bodhisattva spirit: He has a purpose, an intention, a sense of direction, and it is not just for himself; you could call it no-reward action. He comes to China to pass on the living essence of the tradition. This no-reward action might be compared to that of the sun, which shines every day, never thinking to itself, I wish I had never started this. The bodhisattva way is to express your true nature with sincerity in each moment. And that is the essence of Bodhidharma's coming to China.

Now let us look at Hsiang-lin's response in this case. Zen Master

Seung Sahn's translation has him saying, "Sitting for a long time becomes wearisome." There are a few other versions: "Sitting long and getting tired,"[2] and "Sitting for a long time becomes toilsome."[3] But they all come down to the same thing. Hsiang-lin's answer is in the style of Yun-men's short-answer Zen, when he would respond to a question with just one word, or at most only a few. When someone asked Yun-men, "What is it that goes beyond the buddhas and the patriarchs?" Yun-men replied, "Cake." Another time someone asked Yun-men, "What is every-dust-particle samadhi?" *Samadhi* technically means deep meditation, where there is no division between the meditator and what is meditated on; all has become one. "Every dust particle" is similar to the myriad flavors—the world of multiple experiences. So when the monk asked, "What is every-dust-particle samadhi?" Yun-men answers, "Water in the bucket, rice in the bowl."

Here Hsiang-lin is not just aping Yun-men's style like a monkey. He has thoroughly digested this style, assimilated it, and made it his own. When he says, "Sitting for a long time becomes wearisome," he reveals his Zen spirit completely. It is a flavorless, nonthinking statement. It just—*ptchh*—pops out with full presence and full vitality and completely cuts off the thinking of the questioner. A similar situation might be the moment a concert pianist sits down at the piano and hits the first note. There is just a full sense of presence: the piano, the sound, the player are completely one. So here, as Hsiang-lin reveals himself, his answer spontaneously connects with Bodhidharma's Zen, which he of course understood very well. Bodhidharma sat nine years at Shaolin Temple; Hsiang-lin spent eighteen years with Yun-men, who asked only, "What is it?" Hsiang-lin connected spontaneously with Bodhidharma's Zen, with the everyday spirit of Zen. An eminent teacher commenting on this said, "When you sit for a long time your legs hurt: it's nothing special—the eyes are horizontal, the nose vertical; [Hsiang-lin] just lets everyone know that they breathe through their noses."[4] That is Hsiang-lin's everyday spirit of Zen.

In the statement "Sitting for a long time becomes wearisome," you cannot take the word *becomes* in the usual sense. It does not mean that first you sit for a long time, and then tiredness appears. If you think that way, you have before and after; then you have time and space as well as causality, and an idea of doing something to achieve something else. Thinking that way leads to ideas like, I practice Zen to become enlightened. And that kind of idea introduces a big problem. The way Hsiang-lin uses it, *becomes* does not have that connotation. His use of the word suggests that at the time of long sitting, there simply is tired. Long sitting is tired. Tired is long sitting. At the moment you attain long sitting, you attain tired; at the moment of tired, long sitting is not something apart from that. If you see it that way, the true spirit of practice can emerge. True spirit of practice is when sitting, just sitting; when tired, just tired. There is no sense of regret there, no sense of irritation or expectation. That action is all of one piece.

When Hsiang-lin was about to die, he said to the assembled monks, "For forty years long, this monk has been all of one piece." "All of one piece" means that when you do something, you do not have regrets. You do not think, I wish I hadn't started this, or I wish I had tried it some other way. At the time of sitting, there is just sitting. At the time of tired, there is just tired. There is no sense of something other than that. It is complete action.

But that is not always easy to pull off. We often lose that spirit. Sometimes we need something to wake us up to it again. The other day someone told me, "I had an experience where I realized that I wasn't going to live forever." She said that at the time she thought, My daughter is going to do things someday when I won't be there to see them. We all know we are not going to live forever; we even say it from time to time. But we rarely let it really hit us in the middle, in our guts. This person told me, "If I'm not going to live forever, then I had better take seriously what I'm doing just now. Instead of having one foot in and one foot out, I'd better put both feet in." In some traditions, that is called using death as our adviser.

The story of Buddha's leaving the palace and going away to practice tells of a related recognition. In that first step on his journey, the story says, he saw four things he had never seen before: an old person, a sick person, a dead person, and a monk. It is hard to imagine that he had never before seen any of those, but it certainly means that for the first time he really saw them and really allowed that to affect him in an immediate and direct way. Sometimes an experience like that reawakens us to this essential vow of truly acting with sincerity and completeness.

More often, perhaps, we hear stories of the opposite reaction to a brush with death. Another story involved a grown daughter and her mother. The mother was a terrible alcoholic, who kept drinking and drinking until she ruined her health, destroyed her liver, and was close to death. At the eleventh hour, they found a liver transplant for her. Still, after recovering from her surgery, the mother started drinking again, just as she had done before. The daughter said, "What are you doing? You almost died!" The mother responded, "What are you getting so excited about? It's a new liver." We all think that way sometimes.

Another point comes out of this kong-an: Sometimes tiredness is an essential element in spiritual unfolding. At times we need to exhaust ourselves before we believe something. A student once told me, "I have a stream of Zen rhetoric going on in my mind continuously." When it becomes totally absurd and you get complete indigestion from it, you just vomit the whole thing up. For the first time, you recognize that all of this rhetoric really has little to do with your actual experience, and for the first time you attain sincere don't-know.

Several years ago, a man told me a story about a time when he and a friend had exhausted themselves. Throughout his life, this fellow had had difficulty with his weight. He would go on a diet, lose lots of weight, gain it back, and then go through the whole process over and over again. At this particular time he was extremely overweight. He and a friend made a pact to go to Weight Watchers together and start a program one month from that day. Meanwhile they proceeded to eat as much as they could. Back then there were Chinese smorgasbord restaurants in New York. Night after night for a month they frequented these restaurants, completely stuffing themselves. On the last night—the next day was to be their first Weight Watchers meeting— they went to a Carvel ice cream store. At that time, Carvel featured an ice cream log, a substantial piece of cake and ice cream that was meant to serve several people. The two men devoured it, looked at each other, and then agreed, "Phew, thank God that's over." That is one version of the spirit of wearing yourself out.

The Japanese Zen tradition has a story about Zen Master Bankei. As a young man, he studied Confucianism and was exposed to the phrase "bright virtue." He wondered what that meant and asked the Confucian scholars with whom he was studying. But no one could give him a satisfactory answer. Finally one Confucian teacher who was honest with him said, "Actually, we don't really know what that means experientially, but Zen monks concern themselves with things like that. So you should go and ask a Zen monk." When Bankei found a Zen monk and asked about it, the monk told him, "If you want to experience what the bright virtue is, you have to sit zazen."[5] Bankei then began a vigorous program of sitting. He would go into the mountains for several days at a time, climbing up and finding a rock to sit on. He would pull up his robe and sit on the rock with his bare behind, proceeding to sit meditation for many hours, losing himself in it, forgetting to eat, and continuing to sit until he fell over in exhaustion.

After doing this for quite a while, he built a hut in his own village and continued to practice, sitting up all night and not eating. Because of the previous sitting on bare rocks, his skin was irritated and raw, so he began to bleed when he sat. That did not stop him; he just got some cotton batting and continued his rigorous practice. After some time, his body began to break down and he became ill, because there was no sense of balance or moderation in his practice. Friends told him that he needed to recuperate and convalesce. A servant was hired for him, but his condition got progressively worse. Judging from the symptoms described in texts, it appears he had some kind of tubercular condition, because his appetite completely disappeared. He would vomit up a congealed, thick sputum filled with blood. He got to the point where he could not eat at all and began thinking, I'm probably going to die soon. It is said that his only regret about dying was that he had never realized the meaning of the bright virtue.

At this point, he either vomited or had a coughing spell where he spat up a large black chunk of something. When it came out, he suddenly experienced an unusual feeling of openness and clearness in his chest, and felt curiously refreshed. At that moment he realized, Everything is completely managed in the Unborn. I've just been uselessly knocking myself out, because up till today I couldn't see this. After that realization, his style of practice completely changed, and he always advised people to practice gently and easily.

Many years ago, I was a student of Swami Satchidananda, a guru in the Hindu yoga tradition. In a talk, he said, "After all of you people completely exert yourselves, twisting into pretzels through various yoga postures, and holding your breath until you feel like you're going to burst, and repeating mantras thousands upon thousands upon thousands of times, and concentrating on this chakra and that chakra, after you do all this and completely exhaust yourselves, in the end you will just have to completely surrender." That means, in the end you just have to completely let go and put it all down. Sometimes, in order to do that, tiredness becomes a facilitator, but that kind of practice is not necessary if you are not so stubborn and hardheaded.

At the end of this case is a poem. One of the lines reads, "Take off the muzzle, set down the load,"[6] or translated somewhat differently, "Strip off the blinders, unload the saddlebags."[7] That means there is nothing too special about all of this, just that your eyes are horizontal and your nose is vertical. If your action becomes all of one piece, then your mind comes to rest, and then you can be helpful to yourself and to others.

Notes

1. Seung Sahn, trans., *The Blue Cliff Record* (Cumberland, RI: Kwan Um School of Zen, 1983), 14.
2. Frederick Franck, ed., *Zen and Zen Classics: Selections from R.H. Blyth* (New York: Vintage, 1978), 191.
3. Thomas Cleary and J. C. Cleary, trans., *The Blue Cliff Record* (Boston: Shambhala, 1992), 110.
4. Ibid., 114.

5. See Peter Haskel, *Bankei Zen: Translations from the Record of Bankei* (New York: Grove Press, 1984), 11.

6. Franck, 191.

7. Cleary and Cleary, 112.

CHAPTER 18

Tou-shuai's Three Gates

. . . .

Can you attach long or short to the journey?

Is the path wide or narrow?

Is this within time and space or not?

If you digest all of this, then what becomes clear?

Haahh!!

The whole world is one gate, why not come in?

. . . .

Case 47 in the *Wu-men-kuan* (*Mumonkan; Mu Mun Kwan*) says:

Zen Master Tou-shuai made three gates to test his students.

Cutting ignorance grass and sitting Zen is wishing to see nature. Then where is your nature now?

You already understand your nature and pass beyond life and death. When you die, how then will you be reborn?

You already have freedom over life and death and also understand where you return to. When the four elements disperse, where do you go?[1]

Those are Tou-shuai's Three Gates. Then Zen Master Wu-men (Mumon; Mu Mun) follows with this short poem:

Truly perceived one mind numberless kalpas [eons].
Numberless kalpas, these are just now.
Just now see exploded one mind,
See exploded those who just now see.[2]

Wu-men also writes a commentary:

If you can utter three pivotal sayings here, you can be
the master wherever you are; whatever circumstances
you encounter are themselves the source. [That means
in all situations you are in close contact with the essence,
no matter what you are doing.] Otherwise [meaning if
you have not yet reached this stage of development], it is
easy to fill up on coarse food, hard to starve if you chew
thoroughly.[3]

Another translation says, "Gulping down your food will fill you up
quickly, while chewing well will make it more difficult to become hungry again."[4] Clearly he is not talking about rice and beans and french
fries here—he is talking about dharma food, sustaining spiritual food.
If you get some experience quickly and just gulp it down, perhaps that
won't sustain you for long. The essence of practice is slow chewing—
slow development, slow cultivation, and slow unfolding.

Tou-shuai (Tosotsu; To Sal) was a Zen master who lived around
the year 1000. In the lineage of Zen masters stemming from Lin-chi
(Rinzai), he comes toward the end of what is considered the classical
period of Zen in China. Because he died at the early age of forty-
eight and left no successors, his teaching was not passed down to
other teachers. We do, however, have his three gates through which
we attempt to enter.

Each of the three gates is of great interest, but the gates should
not be interesting to us just for the sake of philosophical knowledge. Rather, each one ought to inform our practice from moment to
moment, from day to day.

Tou-shuai's first gate begins by saying, "Cutting ignorance grass and sitting Zen is wishing to see nature." This expression, cutting ignorance grass, literally refers to the hair one shaves off when one becomes a monk or a nun. It means that we are all very attached to appearance and the superficialities of life, and by clinging to appearances we miss something that is more fundamental. So when a monk or a nun shaves off their hair, they are saying, I want to cut my attachment to this narrow, limiting view of myself and perceive something more profound.

In the Zen tradition, you find images like grass, weeds, vines, and creepers. These are metaphors for our habit of getting wrapped up in fixed patterns of perception or behavior as we cling to what we consider to be our egos. For example, Zen Master Ching-ch'ing (Kyosei; Gyeong Cheong) said to a monk who had missed the point in what Ching-ch'ing was saying, "You too are a person caught up in the weeds," meaning that you are caught up in your ideas and don't see what is right in front of you. Actually, even the kong-an collections are often referred to as vines and creepers, suggesting that they might also make complications where originally everything was pure and simple.

In a broader sense, cutting ignorance grass has the connotation of cutting through delusion. That is why the second bodhisattva vow says, "Delusions are endless, I vow to cut through them all." In the case, Tou-shuai says, "Cutting ignorance grass and sitting Zen." Sitting Zen is one side of our practice, but if you think that practice is just sitting Zen, then you are attached to the formality of meditation. Tou-shuai is encouraging us to cut through ignorance and delusion moment by moment in every situation—not just while sitting. In the same way, when we are standing, we should see clearly; when we are eating, we should see clearly; when we are conversing, we should see clearly. Cut ignorance grass moment by moment and sit Zen.

Then he states that these two, cutting off ignorance and sitting Zen, are wishing to see nature. This is a very important sentence. *Nature* here means our fundamental or essential nature. True nature and buddha nature are the same thing. There is an old saying, "Just seeing is buddha nature." Not that you are going to see buddha nature, but the very act of just seeing is buddha nature. When you just see, just hear, just sit, just walk, or just eat, then true nature is already manifested. The word *just* here is important. It sounds simple, but to become simple is not so simple.

Also here, "wishing to see nature" refers to aspiration, our aspiration, toward practice. Why practice? We aspire to perceive our true nature and to understand our correct job in the world. Sometimes we express this by telling ourselves to make a firm determination to attain enlightenment and help others. We frequently hear it said that at the very moment one gives rise to a sincere aspiration for practice, one has the first moment of enlightenment. That is why the phrase "Zen mind, beginner's mind" is so apt.

The term "beginner's mind" comes from the Hua Yen Sutra. The sutra tells a long story about a young pilgrim named Sudhana who goes seeking enlightenment from fifty-three different teachers. When he starts on his journey, the first teacher he comes to is Manjushri (Monju; Mun Su Sari), the Bodhisattva of Primal Wisdom. Manjushri then sends him on a journey to the other fifty-two teachers. After he has passed through all this refinement of practice, he again meets Manjushri. The meaning of this is clearly that where you begin is where you end. The path of practice is the expression of compassion and wisdom as they come together in our activity at the moment. Wishing to see true nature is to give rise to the kind of aspiration that sustains our practice and upon which our practice is based.

After asserting that cutting ignorance grass and sitting Zen is wishing to see nature, Tou-shuai challenges us: "Then where is your nature now?" How is it manifesting just now? This true nature is everything's true nature. It is something that we all share and participate in together. How that is expressing itself is unique and different moment by moment with each one of us. This is why Tou-shuai asks, Where is your true nature just now? This is his first gate.

In the second gate, he goes further to state, "You already understand your nature and pass beyond life and death." You could say, first you understand, then you attain, then you digest and assimilate your understanding and attainment. Since you already understand your true nature, you pass beyond life and death. What does it mean to pass beyond life and death? Some translations say, "You certainly are free from life and death."[5] Tou-shuai goes on to ask, "When you die, how then will you be reborn?"

Life, death, and rebirth: What do those terms mean? There are various ways to look at them. The purpose of the examination is not an intellectual pursuit but one that should strengthen your practice, for we all have to face the moment of death sometime. To pass beyond life and death means you transcend life and death. When you come to the moment before thought, you and the universe become one. To become one doesn't mean that before you weren't one and now you have become one (already from the beginning you were one with the universe), but at that moment you recognize that you and the universe are completely one, never separate. If you and the universe are already one, there is no life and no death. Life and death are like putting on your clothes in the morning and taking them off at night or driving your car for a long time until it won't go anymore and leaving it in the junk heap and getting a new car. Fundamentally there is no coming and no going. But lest you make the assumption that no coming or going means there must be something permanent, another sutra says, "No coming, no going, and no abiding." That means no staying either.

Transcending life and death means in one sense transcending the distinctions we make, the artificial demarcation line we make between something we call life and something we call death. In the Zen tradition, to pass beyond something or to be free of it does not mean that you have escaped it—you don't go to the pure land or some heaven where there is no life or death. To transcend life and death means at the moment of life, there is just life, and at the moment of death, there is just death.

Sometimes in the Zen tradition we talk about life and death or birth and death as the moment-to-moment appearing and disappearing of things in our mind. If you sit meditation and watch your mind, you see that thinking comes, thinking goes, feeling arises, feeling passes away, sensation appears, sensation disappears. All this coming and going moment by moment is sometimes called birth and death. To pass beyond birth and death means to not be caught up and cling to the momentary forms of your mind's fluctuations. It also means you don't push them away or reject them. When you can just be with whatever is, moment by moment, you transcend life and death.

Also in Zen, life and death refers to holding and clinging versus letting go. There is a famous Zen saying: "The act of a great person is, when hanging over a cliff a thousand feet in the air, to let go." You let go into open boundless being that is clear like space. Is that life or is that death? Sometimes what looks like death is becoming alive, and what looks like dying is being born. Also, to die refers to the moment when we let go of our small, contracted, egocentric view. At that moment, we achieve what is referred to as the Great Death, which means we have an enlightenment experience. In that experience, one side is like death, but the other side is like emerging into something new—rebirth.

In Zen poetry, you often find expressions such as:

Flowers bloom on a withered tree in a spring beyond kalpas;
you ride a jade elephant backwards, chasing a winged
dragon-deer.[6]

The first line refers to death and rebirth: letting go of small self, becoming big self, open self, becoming more than you conceived of yourself as being.

I have a friend who is fond of the saying, "You're not just your story." We tell ourselves a story about who and what we are so much of the time, and then we identify with that story line. We believe it and begin to fabricate a whole universe around ourselves to substantiate it. But when you come into the clarity of this moment, you recognize that you are not just your story—there is more to it than that. If you experience that kind of freedom, then being occurs without hindrance. In the Lotus Sutra, it says the Bodhisattva of Compassion appears in many different forms—man, woman, layperson, householder, monk, nun, dog, cat, demon. If you understand your true position, and you can connect with the situation moment by moment without holding on to your patterns, then you can adapt and appear according to what is needed.

In the early days of the Providence Zen Center, a small group of people lived in a house in the city with Zen Master Seung Sahn. It was in a very poor neighborhood. In this neighborhood lived a boy around eight years of age who would periodically sneak through the window of the Zen Center and pilfer things. One day Zen Master Seung Sahn was in the garden when this little boy appeared. Suddenly Seung Sahn howled loudly and charged at the boy. The boy was petrified and ran away. Later one of the students said to the Zen master, "I don't know if that was the right kind of action to do." Seung Sahn replied, "Sometimes a demon is necessary." His point was that he saved the boy from being a thief by scaring him away. When you die, how will you be reborn? Not just when you leave this body, but moment by moment how will you manifest yourself according to situations, according to circumstances, according to time and place, and how will you supply what is needed?

This whole notion of dying and being reborn brings up the issues of karma and reincarnation, which are fascinating subjects for some people when they first come in contact with Buddhism. If, however, you are too focused on the notion of reincarnation and rebirth, then the focus of your practice may lean into the future, rather than being directed toward this moment.

Many stories about death are told in the Zen tradition. You can read stories where a Zen master announces to the assembly, "Tomorrow I'll be leaving you." The next day he puts on his robes, shaves his head, sits up in meditation, and quietly dies. But there is also a story of Zen Master Lung-t'an (Ryutan; Yong Dam) who, when he was dying, repeatedly yelled out in agony on his deathbed. His students tried to ease his pain in some way. One version of the story claims that he kept shouting, "It hurts! It hurts!" and so the students tried to stop his pain. Lung-t'an stopped his yells and said, "Don't think that my agony now is in any way different from what my joy and exuberance was." Then he died.

A man said to Zen Master Bankei, "I'm getting on in years. What kind of preparation should I make for my death?" Bankei replied, "No preparation is necessary." The man was surprised because the common Buddhist viewpoint would be that you practice something to get ready for your death. Often laypeople in East Asian countries repeat the name of the Pure Land buddha, Na Mu Amita Bul, to get ready for death. But Bankei said, "No preparation is necessary." So the man asked why, to which Bankei stated, "When you die, just die." This is Bankei's practice connected with death and rebirth.

Tou-shuai's third gate says, "You already have freedom over life and death and also understand where you return to." If you can be reborn in the moment according to circumstances, letting go of self-centered ideas and becoming one with the situation, then you have complete freedom. Moment by moment, everything reveals true nature. Emerging and returning are only superficial changes. As is stated in the Heart Sutra, essentially there is no origination. The process of coming from and returning to is called nature origination. This is why Tou-shuai asks, "Where is your nature now?"

"You understand where you return to. When the four elements disperse, where do you go?" The four elements, according to ancient Indian ideas, are earth, water, fire, and air. From a narrow viewpoint, the four elements mean your physical body, so when your physical body falls apart, where do you go? But the four elements appear in gross and subtle form—we all are constructing our own versions of reality moment by moment and making them out of elements of imagination. When you cut through delusion and the clinging quality of opinion, conception, and idea, at that moment—*ptchh*—the elements disperse. At that point, where do you go? What is your direction? What is your true job? Tou-shuai encourages us to see, perceive, and practice that.

Zen Master Wu-men's poem connected with the kong-an says:

Truly perceived one mind numberless kalpas.
Numberless kalpas, these are just now.

Just now see exploded one mind,
See exploded those who just now see.

The language of Zen Master Seung Sahn's translation is somewhat unusual. A different translation, given by Japanese Roshi Shibayama, elucidates the kong-an a little differently:

This one instant, as it is, is an infinite number of kalpas.
An infinite number of kalpas are at the same time this
    one instant.
If you see into this fact,
The True Self which is seeing has been seen into.[7]

If you grasp this moment, then you grasp just what you are. This poem is based on the philosophy of the Hua Yen Sutra, but it is very practice oriented, because what is emphasized is moment, this instant, just now. Moment means experiencing something wholly and completely. At that point, there is just this moment, no coloration by some idea of the past through memory, no coloration by some imagined sense of what the future is going to bring, but just wholly and completely doing something now, at this instant.

We operate in two kinds of time, but unfortunately we usually only identify and relate to one of them. There is chronological time, with past, present, and future, which we use as demarcations. But where is the past? Where is the present? Where is the future? It is something like watching action on a film strip move from the past to the present to the future. If, however, we look at just one frame, that one mind instant, that one frame of experience just now is complete. Each frame is a complete picture and is related to everything that has preceded it. It also contains everything that will emerge out of it. Without thinking of past or future, in that moment we become completely unified. We just do something. We just act completely. Unfortunately we usually identify ourselves with notions of past, present, and future. But when we bring past, present, and future into our activity, our activity is never clean and complete—it is always colored or tainted.

A friend of mine once sat a retreat with Robert Aitken Roshi in Hawaii. One day, as the bell was hit to end the sitting period, when one is expected to stand up for walking meditation, Aitken Roshi said, "Now, get up and walk with nothing sticking to it." Nothing sticking to it means moment time—don't drag along some memory with you as you walk just now. That is a very important point for practice, because if you look at practice as having past, present, and future, then you can also make comparisons such as, "Yesterday my meditation was pretty good; today it didn't feel so good. Maybe tomorrow it'll be better, and next week I'll get enlightenment." Bringing in these ideas orients your practice toward getting someplace (which is not the place you are now) at some time in the future, or attaining some state that is different from your most immediate state. That becomes a big obstacle to just being and expressing yourself. That is why the Buddha said, "From the beginning, each and every thing already has the awakened nature." He did not say that you will get somewhere sometime, as if practices will manufacture the awakened nature.

If you don't generate time as an idea, then you just act completely. Just sitting, just questioning, just walking, whatever you're doing is not colored by ideation. Practice should be rooted there. In truth, the only freedom we have is there, because as soon as you have an idea of past and future and somewhere to get to, you can never be free. You are always bound by some attempt to move toward something that you are not now. But at the point when you are being in this moment, cleanly and clearly, you find true freedom—not freedom to get away from something or to get away with something but the true freedom of your essential being. At the moment that you act cleanly and clearly you perceive the true relationship of things and understand your connection to the immediate situation.

A poem that is read during the death ceremony in the Korean Zen tradition distills many of the essential points of Hua Yen philosophy:

In one is all
In many is one
One is identical to all
Many is identical to one
In one dust particle is contained the ten directions
And so it is with all particles of dust
Incalculably long eons are identical to a single thought instant
A single thought instant is identical to incalculably long eons
The nine times and the ten directions are mutually identical
Yet are not confused or mixed but function separately
The moment one begins to aspire with their heart
Instantly perfect enlightenment is attained
Samsara and nirvana are always harmonized together.

Someone asked Zen Master Pai-chang (Hyakujo; Baek Jang), "Does the enlightened person come under cause and effect or not?" Pai-chang said, "Cause and effect are not obscured. Cause and effect are clear." It is important to see that past, present, and future are not obscured. Equally important is to see that this moment of freedom is also not obscured.

Notes

1. See Seung Sahn, trans., *The Mu Mun Kwan* (Cumberland, RI: Kwan Um School of Zen, 1983), 55.
2. Ibid.
3. Thomas Cleary, trans., *No Barrier* (New York: Bantam, 1993), 204.
4. Koun Yamada, trans., *The Gateless Gate* (Boston: Wisdom, 2004), 220.
5. Zenkei Shibayama, *The Gateless Barrier* (Boston: Shambhala, 2000), 316.
6. Robert Aitken, *The Morning Star* (Washington, DC: Shoemaker & Hoard, 2003), 152.
7. Shibayama, 316.

CHAPTER 19

Manjushri's Before Three, Three

At this point, can you perceive the non-abiding basis
of enlightened wisdom . . . or not?

In seeing and hearing, in shapes and sounds, can you
perceive the varied teaching of enlightened wisdom . . . or not?

At this point, are variation and oneness the same or different?
Are enlightenment and illusion two or one?

Look!!

A rabbit in the moonlight gives birth to many offspring.

The essence of this kong-an, which is case 35 in *The Blue Cliff Record,* is given in this introduction:

Determining dragons and snakes, distinguishing jewels and stones, separating the profound and the naive, to settle all uncertainty: if you haven't an eye on your forehead [the wisdom eye] and a talisman under your elbow, time and again you will miss the point immediately. Right at this very moment seeing and hearing are not obscured, sound and form are purely real. Tell me, is it black? Is it white? Is it crooked? Is it straight? At this point, how will you discriminate?[1]

And now for the kong-an:

> Manjushri asked Wu Cho, "Where are you coming from?"
> Wu Cho said, "The south."
> Manjushri said, "How is the Buddhist teaching being carried on in the south?"
> Wu Cho said, "At the end of the dharma (the end of the world), only a few monks keep the precepts."
> Manjushri said, "How many assemblies?"
> Wu Cho said, "Some three hundred, some five hundred."
> Wu Cho asked Manjushri, "How is practice being carried on hereabouts?"
> Manjushri said, "Ordinary people and saints live together; dragons and snakes mix."
> Wu Cho said, "How many assemblies?"
> Manjushri said, "Before three, three. After three, three."[2]

Chogyam Trungpa Rinpoche, a Tibetan teacher who founded a group of centers called the Dharmadhatus and taught in the United States for many years, once was asked, What is the difference between Zen Buddhism and Tibetan Tantric Buddhism? He said it was something like the difference between a black-and-white movie and a movie in Technicolor. One of the things that remark points to is that Zen makes use of the ordinary, whereas Tibetan Tantric Buddhism makes use of the miraculous. In Tibetan Buddhism, you find unusual practices: visualizations of various kinds, special breathing exercises, focusing on mystic centers, practices for dying, practices for being reborn. These are all Technicolor kinds of practices. Zen does not emphasize many of these. Instead there are just white walls, brown floors, gray robes, and brown *kasas*. The incautious, inquisitive Zen student may be enjoined to go have a cup of tea. But there are always exceptions to the rule, and this particular case is one.

The two protagonists here are a monk named Wu-cho (Mujaku; Mu Chak) and Manjushri (Monju; Mun Su Sari). Wu-cho was a Zen master who lived in China from about 821 to 900. As a student of Zen Master Yang-shan (Kyozan; An Sahn), he is recorded as coming from one of the early schools of Zen, the Kuei-yang school. His name, Wu-cho, which was given to him by the emperor, means "no attachment," so he must have been a good teacher. That is all we know about him.

The existence of Manjushri is more ambiguous and complex: Can we say he is real or illusory? Or both real and illusory? Or neither real nor illusory?

In the Mahayana Buddhist sutra tradition, various qualities of the enlightened mind—such as compassion, wisdom, great action, great determination or vow—are represented through the figures of the bodhisattvas. The word *bodhisattva* means "enlightening being," so the mind of enlightenment that radiates into action in the world is represented as various bodhisattvas. From the Zen standpoint, however, if you want to find the Bodhisattva of Wisdom, Manjushri, or the Bodhisattva of Compassion, Avalokiteshvara (Kuan-yin; Kannon; Kwan Seum Bosal), you have to look into your own mind.

From this perspective, Manjushri is none other than yourself. But in Mahayana Buddhism, mind is not something limited to the bony cage of your skull; mind is wide, vast, expansive, and extensive. Sights, sounds, experiences, dogs, cats, the various things we encounter, all can offer expressions of the bodhisattva's teaching of compassion or wisdom or determination. Even the person who insults you might be a manifestation of the Bodhisattva of Compassion as well as the Bodhisattva of Wisdom!

A Japanese story tells of Manjushri's wisdom manifesting in an unusual way. Several centuries ago, a great samurai came to a Zen master and asked him, "Is there heaven and hell?" The Zen master replied, "Of course there is heaven and hell." So the samurai said, "I want to see heaven and hell. Can you reveal heaven and hell to me?" The Zen master replied, "Well, I could reveal heaven and hell, but it takes someone of outstanding ability and quality to be able to perceive them." The samurai sat up a little straighter. Then the Zen master said, "You, on the other hand, are quite an inferior being. So it is not possible for you to see heaven and hell." The samurai put his hand on the hilt of his sword. The Zen master continued, "In fact, it would be more likely that a dog could be taught the meaning of heaven and hell than you." In a rage, the samurai—*shhhzzzt!*—pulled out his sword and held it above the Zen master's head. The Zen master said, "Here you enter the gates of hell." At that moment the warrior realized he had been caught and sheathed his sword. The Zen master said, "Here you enter the gates of heaven."

As a young monk, Wu-cho traveled extensively throughout China on a pilgrimage to visit various teachers and temples. When he arrived at Mount Wutai, considered to be the holy site of the Bodhisattva of Wisdom, Manjushri, evening was falling. As he climbed through a rough, wooded area toward the top of the mountain, he realized that he had to find a place to stay. Just then he came upon a clearing, and in that clearing was a temple. The abbot of the temple invited him to come in and stay the night. Then they began to talk. The abbot asked Wu-cho, "Where are you coming from?" and Wu-cho said, "The south." The abbot then asked, "How is the Buddhist teaching being carried on in the south?" Wu-cho said, "At the end of the dharma (end of the world), only a few monks keep the precepts." Then the abbot asked, "How many assemblies?" Wu-cho said, "Some three hundred, some five hundred."

Wu-cho asked the abbot, "How is practice being carried on hereabouts?" The abbot said, "Ordinary people and saints live together; dragons and snakes mix." Wu-cho said, "How many assemblies?" The abbot said, "Before three, three. After three, three." Then tea was served.

As they were having tea, the abbot held up a clear crystal bowl and asked Wu-cho, "Do they also have this in the south?" Wu-cho said, "No." The abbot asked, "Then what do you use to drink tea with?" Wu-cho had no answer. A crystal bowl is something clear and uncolored, completely untainted. If red comes, the crystal just reflects red; if white comes, the crystal reflects white. So a crystal bowl is an image representing clear mind. If you are really going to drink tea and taste the tea, then you need to meet the tea with your mind clear—with no preconceived taste, no taint.

Shortly thereafter they retired for the night.

In the morning, the abbot had his attendant, a young boy, take Wu-cho to the gate of the temple. When they got to the gate portal, Wu-cho said to the boy, "Last night when we were talking, the abbot said, 'Before three, three. After three, three.' How many is that?" The boy suddenly called out, "Oh, monk!" Wu-cho said, "Yes?" And the young boy asked, "How many is this?" Wu-cho was bewildered and had no answer. He asked, "What temple is this?" The boy silently pointed to the mountain behind the temple. Wu-cho turned his head and looked up toward the mountain. When he turned his head back, the boy, the temple, everything had completely vanished. There was just an empty valley. At that moment Wu-sho suddenly realized that Manjushri himself had produced it all.

Later Wu-cho served as the cook of a temple on the same mountain. Every day as he was cooking the rice, Manjushri would appear in the steam above the rice pot. Wu-cho would take the stirrer and hit Manjushri—*puk*—and Manjushri would disappear. But Zen Master Yuan-wu said, "Still, this is drawing the bow after the thief has left." That means too late. Wu-cho should have hit the abbot (Manjushri) when he asked how practice was in the south![3]

That is one of the miracle stories of Chinese Zen, and it serves as the background of this case. If we go back into the case line by line, we find a number of interesting and important points. When Manjushri asks Wu-cho, "Where are you coming from?" he is asking a fundamental Zen question. Sometimes it is translated as, Where have you come from most recently? Or, Where have you come from just now? Where are you coming from? encompasses the absolute, the relative, and this moment.

Here is an everyday example of that combination: Water in certain conditions becomes ice; ice in certain conditions becomes steam; steam in certain conditions becomes water. Likewise our experience in the world is based on particular causes and supporting conditions, moment by moment. We interact in various ways with situations and people; we unfold in various ways. In Buddhism that is called our *karma*; it points to the fact that all things are impermanent and are changing rapidly. This is the principle of dependent origination.

In the relative world of our experience, everything is supported by something else. Who we are depends on many things—things we do not usually consider to be part of ourselves. Similarly water comes from H_2O, ice comes from H_2O, and steam comes from H_2O. The fundamental nature of water, steam, and ice—all of them—is H_2O. You cannot, however, find H_2O anywhere but in water, steam, or ice. You cannot grab hold of something called H_2O without grabbing water, steam, or ice.

In Zen we look into ourselves and recognize that there is some fundamental nature that is the nonabiding basis of who we are, moment by moment by moment. We are always coming from that, and we are always supported by that. We are never apart from that. It is our nature. That means that in each moment everything is complete: no before, no after, no present even. There is just this moment.

Here is a story about, Where are you coming from?

Zen Master Fa-yen (Hogen; Poep An) asked Elder Jiao, "Did you come by boat or by land?" Jiao said, "By boat." Fa-yen said, "Where is the boat?" Jiao said, "The boat is on the water." After Jiao had withdrawn, Fa-yen turned and asked a monk standing by, "You tell me, did that monk just now have eyes or not?"[4] Did he see the point of what I was getting at or not?

A similar situation occurred once when I was visiting a temple in Korea with colleagues from the Kwan Um School of Zen. The temple's abbot asked one of our monks, "Did you come by boat or by plane?" Not realizing he was being engaged in dharma combat at that moment, the monk replied, "We came by plane." Then Zen Master Seung Sahn, who was sitting next to him, pointed to the door. The monk looked, then said, "Oh! Just now I came from the door." Not plane, not boat, but just now from the door.

It helps to know that in Buddhist imagery the body-mind is referred to as the boat that will carry us across. Sometimes the teaching, the dharma, is also referred to as a boat that carries us across. In one of the sutras, Buddha tells a parable suggesting that once you cross the river with a boat, you do not keep carrying the boat on your head; you leave it in the river and continue on your way.

When the monk answered Zen Master Fa-yen, "I came by boat," the Zen master challenged him one more time: "Where is the boat?" The monk said in the most ordinary way, "The boat is on the river." Where else would it be? The monk's answer is either high class in the guise of ordinariness, or he has not gotten the point at all, leading Zen Master Fa-yen to ask afterward, "Did that monk have eyes or not?" A comment on that particular story says: "In mundane truth, how many people have been enlightened, in Buddhist truth, how many people have become deluded! If they suddenly become one, can you then define delusion or enlightenment?"[5]

A story about the Sixth Patriarch, Hui-neng (E'no) makes a similar point. As a young man, Hui-neng was an illiterate woodcutter in the south of China. One day as he was delivering wood, he heard a monk chanting a sutra with the line, "Not abiding anywhere, let the mind come forth." Upon hearing that line, he had some kind of opening experience and asked the monk, "What is that scripture you are chanting there? And where did you learn it?" The monk said, "This is the Diamond Sutra, and I learned it from the Fifth Patriarch at Hong Mei."

Hui-neng decided to travel there and meet the Fifth Patriarch. He traveled on foot; it was a long way. When he got there, the Fifth Patriarch asked, "Where are you coming from, and what do you seek here?" Hui-neng said, "I've come from the south, and I don't seek anything. I just want to realize my buddha nature." The Fifth Patriarch poked at him a little and said, "How can you barbarians from the south realize your buddha nature?" Hui-neng replied, "In ordinary terms there may be south and north, but in the buddha nature, there is no such thing. You and I may be of different social class, but in the buddha nature do any of those things exist or not?" The Fifth Patriarch realized that this was an unusual student.[6]

When Manjushri asked, "How is the Buddhist teaching being carried out in the south?"—How is it being carried out in your part of the world?—Wu-cho said that at the end of the dharma, in that deteriorating age, only a few monks were keeping the precepts. That is only shop talk. How is practice being carried out in the south, how is practice being carried out in your part of the world, means how is your practice. "Your part of the world" means you. Is your practice strong, is your practice steady, is your practice weak? Show me, just now. But Wu-cho misses the point entirely.

Manjushri, indulging him one more time, asks, "How many assemblies are there?" And Wu-cho says, "Some three hundred, some five hundred." But "how many assemblies" means, the many are the one, the one are the many. It points back to you. What kind of assembly are you? How many assemblies right here and now? That means, do not look at how anyone else is practicing. How are you practicing? If twenty-five people show up to practice—wonderful! If one and a half show up for practice—wonderful! How are you practicing today?

Manjushri's question, "How many assemblies?" might be compared to the question Zen Master Kuei-shan (Isan; Wi Sahn) asked his student Yang-shan (Kyozan; An Sahn): "Where have you been?" When Yang-shan answered, "I have just come from the field," Kuei-shan asked, "How many people are there?" Yang-shan thrust his hoe into the ground and stood there motionless. Kuei-shan said, "Today on the southern mountain a man worked at harvesting the rushes." Thereupon Yang-shan picked up his hoe and began to walk away.[7] That is "How many people? How many assemblies?" If you think about how many people, you are relating to the world as if it were outside of you. But essentially there is no inside, no outside, no many, no few. That is all conceptualization, all secondary.

When Wu-cho turns the tables on Manjushri, asking, "How is practice being carried on hereabouts?" Manjushri gives an interesting answer. First he says, "Ordinary people and saints live together; dragons and snakes mix." If you look into your mind with attentiveness, exactitude, openness, and calmness, you will soon see ordinary people and saints dwelling together; demons, gods, the whole array appear. If you look again, you will see dragons and snakes mixing together. Dragons are powerful; snakes are not so powerful. One moment you may feel strong; the next moment you may not feel so strong. But if you do not check any of that, do not hold on to any of that, do not attach to any of that, then it is just the unfolding of your mind, moment by moment: ordinary people and saints dwelling together, dragons and snakes intermingling. This is our practice.

But Wu-cho did not understand what Manjushri was pointing to, so he asked, "How many assemblies?" Manjushri answered in an interesting way: "Before three, three; after three, three." The next morning Wu-cho asked the boy, "How many is before three, three, after three, three?

There is a Zen saying: One by one, each thing is complete. One by one, each thing has it. When Wu-cho asked the boy how many that was—before three, three, after three, three—the boy called out, "Oh, monk!" Calling is complete. Then, without thinking at all, Wu-cho said, "Yes." That is answering is complete. Calling is complete, answering is complete. Drinking tea is complete. Keeping the precepts is complete; also breaking the precepts is complete. That means why do you do anything that you do? What is your intention? If you let go of self-preoccupation, then you connect with the world right before you. If you connect with the world before you without excessive self-preoccupation, then compassionate activity is possible, wisdom perception is possible, skillful action is possible.

Zen Master Pai-chang (Hyakujo; Baek Jang) once addressed the assembly: "Not setting in motion good or evil, right or wrong [not imposing onto your experience some notion of good and bad, or right and wrong], not clinging to a single thing, not rejecting a single thing [an important point] . . . ." Sometimes people view spiritual practice as detachment, letting go of everything, stepping back in some way. But here Zen Master Pai-chang presents two sides: not clinging to anything, also not rejecting anything. That is true openness. Dragons come, dragons. Snakes come, snakes. Saints come, saints. Ordinary people come, ordinary people. No problem.

Zen Master Pai-chang continued, "This is called being a member of the Great Caravan." That is before three, three. After three, three.

Notes

1. Thomas Cleary and J. C. Cleary, trans., *The Blue Cliff Record* (Boston: Shambhala, 1992), 216.

2. Seung Sahn, trans., *The Blue Cliff Record* (Cumberland, RI: Kwan Um School of Zen, 1983), 30.

3. See Cleary and Cleary, 216–20.

4. See Thomas Cleary, trans., *Book of Serenity* (Boston: Shambhala, 1988), 215.

5. Ibid.

6. See Zenkei Shibayama, *The Gateless Barrier* (Boston: Shambhala, 2000), 167–68.

7. See Chang Chung-yuan, trans., *Original Teachings of Ch'an Buddhism* (New York: Grove Press, 1995), 185–86.

CHAPTER 20

Vimalakirti's Not-Two Dharma Gate

Look. Listen. When you see colors or hear sounds, is that
an experience of one or two?

When you see colors or hear sounds, don't say, "One," don't say, "Two."

Not one, not two. Then what?

Haahh!!

2 x 2 = 4. 1 x 1 = 1.

"Vimalakirti's Not-Two Dharma Gate," case 84 in *The Blue Cliff Record*, offers us a challenging kong-an that leads toward deepening the experience of the power of silence. It says:

Vimalakirti asked Manjushri, "What is a bodhisattva's entry into the not-two dharma gate?"

Manjushri said, "According to what I think, in all dharmas, no words, no speech, no revelation, and no understanding, to let go all questions and answers: This is entering the not-two dharma gate."

Then Manjushri asked Vimalakirti, "We have each already spoken. Now you should tell us, good man, what is a bodhisattva's entry into the not-two dharma gate?"[1]

Hsueh-tou (Setcho), the compiler of these cases, then wrote, "What did Vimalakirti say?" He also wrote, "Completely exposed."[2]

This kong-an appears in both *The Blue Cliff Record* and *Book of Serenity*. Each collection has a few introductory remarks. *The Blue Cliff Record* says, "Though you say 'It is,' there is nothing which 'is' can affirm. Though you say 'It is not,' there is nothing that 'is not' can negate. When 'is' and 'is not' are left behind, and gain and loss are forgotten, then you are clean and naked, free and at ease."[3] In its introduction to the kong-an, *Book of Serenity* says, "Even if one's eloquence is unhindered, there's a time when one can't open one's mouth."[4]

A few remarks are needed on the wording of this case: first, the title, "Not-Two Dharma Gate." Is "not-two" negating something? What is it that is not two? When Vimalakirti asked Manjushri (Monju; Mun Su Sari), "What is a bodhisattva's entry into the not-two dharma gate?" and Manjushri replied, "According to what I think, in all dharmas, no words, no speech," what is the meaning of *dharma*? In Sanskrit, *dharma* has several meanings. One connotation is "truth," so we think of the buddha, the dharma, and the sangha, with *dharma* meaning impersonal truth. But another meaning is the teaching. Sometimes we talk about the buddha dharma—Buddha's teaching. Yet, any phenomenal occurrence, any momentary experience we have, may also be called a dharma, in recognition that anything we experience moment by moment in the phenomenal world is a teaching of some kind.

Here, Manjushri's use of the word is plural, "in all dharmas." Essentially he is saying that entering the not-two dharma gate means relating to all things, yet clearly perceiving your experiences as outside the province of words and speech; relating to things as not revealing anything, without trying to understand anything; accepting all your experiences without questions, without answers.

One ancient commentator said that Manjushri's comments here are something like a tortoise who comes out of the ocean, walks up on the beach, digs a hole, plants her eggs, then walks back down toward the water, swinging her tail back and forth to wipe out her footprints. Unfortunately the tail itself leaves marks that reveal where the eggs are buried. Manjushri says, "In all things, no words, no speech." But he has already said something, so he leaves a trail; it is not completely clean. Another commentator said, "Manjushri doesn't have any ground to stick a digging tool into, but Vimalakirti doesn't even have a digging tool."[5]

This interchange between Manjushri and Vimalakirti comes from one of the Buddhist sutras. In the kong-an, when Manjushri asks Vimalakirti, "What is the bodhisattva's entry into the not-two dharma gate?" Hsueh-tou asks, "What did Vimalakirti say?" But in the sutra, when Manjushri asks Vimalakirti to speak on the not-two dharma gate, Vimalakirti does not say anything—there is just complete, profound silence.

In a similar story, when the national teacher was quite old, the emperor of China asked him, "When you pass on, what will you need?" The national teacher said, "Build me a seamless monument." The emperor was confused, because he didn't know what a seamless monument could be, so he said, "Master, the monument's form?" The national teacher just sat quietly for a while, then asked the emperor, "Understand?" The emperor said he did not.

On another occasion, Zen Master Wu-tsu (Goso; Oh Jo) addressed the assembly and said, "When you meet a master on the road, don't greet him with speech, don't greet him with silence." All these examples raise a question in our practice: What is true silence versus an attachment to quietness?

A student who had not been practicing for very long once said to me. "I think I'd like to do a retreat pretty soon." I told her, "That's a good idea. We're going to have a three-day retreat here in the Zen Center in New York soon." She replied, "Oh, if I do a retreat, I need to go to the country somewhere, up in the mountains." I realized she had not yet understood the essence of what constitutes true silence. That is a very important point—what is true silence versus attachment to quietness? Vimalakirti's silence in the face of Manjushri's question is sometimes referred to as the "great roar of Vimalakirti's silence." It was not passive silence.

This case comes from the Vimalakirti Sutra, which has the alternate title "The Dharma Door of Inconceivable Liberation." What is inconceivable liberation? It is what we call don't-know. If you can conceive of it, you know it. If you cannot conceive of it, it is only not knowing.

Before looking further into this sutra, however, it may be helpful to consider a few things about sutras in general. They are part of the scriptural canon of Buddhism. The word *sutra* literally means "thread." While sutras present threads of different kinds of teaching, they do not elaborate these teachings into a fully evolved philosophical system of any kind. Sutras may mix together teachings on emptiness, teachings on all things are made by mind, all things are interpenetrating, within the small is contained the big, within the near is contained the far, within the present is contained the past and future. And in these sutras, none of the teachings obstruct each other. You can also find sutra teachings about meditation, compassion, and giving.

Usually the main character in the sutras is the Buddha, who is teaching his followers. Occasionally he tells parables, or a miracle occurs to let you know that you are not in the world of ordinary, everyday experience.

But in the sutra we are considering here, the main character is Vimalakirti, a layman and wealthy merchant who is also considered a high-level bodhisattva, almost equal to the Buddha himself. The teaching goes on between Vimalakirti, other bodhisattvas, and the Buddha's main disciples, including Mahakashyapa, Shariputra, and Rahula. While these disciples are portrayed as having significant attainment in formal meditation and the orthodox practices of keeping the precepts, they still cling to some dualistic ideas. The disciples are frequently caught by ideas of purity versus impurity, this world versus the quiet and cessation of nirvana, the orthodox practices versus something prohibited; they are hindered by all these attachments. The bodhisattvas, on the other hand, are portrayed in the sutra as having a practice that is open, altruistic, compassionate, wide, nondualistic, and nonclinging, and these two types of attitudes are repeatedly contrasted. The character of Shariputra is used as a main foil to reveal this contrast. Vimalakirti keeps focusing on Shariputra and poking at the narrow view he holds. In the service of dislodging concepts, a lot of verbal jousting takes place, which is one reason it was highly valued by the Zen sect.

Here is an example of Vimalakirti confronting Shariputra about the true nature of practice.

> At that time Vimalakirti approached and said to me, "Ah, Shariputra, you should not assume that this form of sitting is true quiet sitting! Quiet sitting means that in this threefold world you manifest neither body nor will [neither body nor mind]. This is quiet sitting. Not rising out of your samadhi [deep meditation] of complete cessation and yet showing yourself in the ceremonies of daily life—this is quiet sitting. Not abandoning the principles of the Way and yet showing yourself in the activities of a common mortal—this is quiet sitting. Your mind not fixed on internal things and yet not engaged with externals either—this is quiet sitting. Unmoved by sundry theories, but practicing the thirty-seven elements of the Way—this is quiet sitting. Entering nirvana without having put an end to earthly desires—this is quiet sitting. If you can do this kind of sitting, you will merit the Buddha's seal of approval."[6]

Similar remarks about true meditation can be seen in the well-known exchange between Ma-tsu (Baso; Ma Jo) and his teacher Nan-yueh Huai-jang (Nangaku). Once when Ma-tsu was sitting in meditation, Huai-jang walked by and said, "What are you doing?" Ma-tsu responded, "I'm sitting to become Buddha." Huai-jang picked up a tile from the ground and began rubbing it. Ma-tsu said, "What are you doing?" Huai-jang told him, "I'm polishing this tile to turn it into a mirror." Ma-tsu said, "No matter how much you polish a tile, it will never become a mirror." Huai-jang shot back, "No matter how much sitting you do, you will never become Buddha." Ma-tsu became confused and told his master that he did not understand. Huai-jang replied, "If you're riding in a cart, do you hit the horse or the cart?" Ma-tsu still didn't understand, so Huai-jang said, "Are you sitting in meditation, or are you sitting to become Buddha? If you are sitting in meditation, you should know that essentially meditation is neither sitting nor lying. And if you're sitting to become Buddha, Buddha has no particular fixed form. If you practice the nonabiding dharma, then you should neither reject nor cling to anything. If you are sitting to become Buddha, then you are just killing the Buddha."[7]

What follows in the sutra is a dialogue between Shariputra and an enlightened goddess. Their discussion centers on essential identity as contrasted with gender identity. Shariputra asks the goddess why she doesn't change out of her female body. At that time in India, the notion was that women could not attain complete enlightenment—the most a woman could hope for was to practice, gain merit, and be born in her next life as a man who could then achieve great enlightenment. The goddess says:

> "For the past twelve years, I have been trying to take on female form, but in the end with no success [meaning that in essential nature there is no male or female]. What is there to change? If a sorcerer were to conjure up a phantom woman and then someone asked her why she didn't change out of her female body, would that be any kind of reasonable question?"
>
> "No," said Shariputra. "Phantoms have no fixed form, so what would there be to change?"
>
> The goddess said, "All things are just the same—they have no fixed form. So why ask why I don't change out of my female form?"
>
> At that time the goddess employed her supernatural powers to change Shariputra into a goddess like herself, while she took on Shariputra's form. Then she asked, "Why don't you change out of this female body?"
>
> Shariputra, now in the form of a goddess, replied, "I don't know why I have changed and suddenly taken on this female body!"
>
> The goddess said, "Shariputra, if you can change out

of this female body, then all women can change likewise. Shariputra, who is not a woman, appears in a woman's body. And the same is true of all women—though they appear in women's bodies, they are not women. Therefore the Buddha teaches that all phenomena are neither male nor female."

Then the goddess withdrew her supernatural powers, and Shariputra returned to his original form. The goddess said to Shariputra, "Where now is the form and shape of your female body?"

Shariputra said, "The form and shape of my female body does not exist, yet does not not exist."

The goddess said, "All things are just like that—they do not exist, yet they do not not exist. And that they do not exist, yet do not not exist, is exactly what the Buddha teaches."[8]

Don't say this, don't say that. A Zen teacher might hold up her stick and say, "If you call this a Zen stick, you are attached to name and form. If you say it is not a Zen stick, you are attached to emptiness. Is this a Zen stick or not?"

Somewhat later, Vimalakirti says to all the various bodhisattvas who are present, "Sirs, how does the bodhisattva go about entering the gate of nondualism [the not-two dharma gate]? Let each one explain as he understands it."[9]

Each bodhisattva says a little something. The bodhisattva Virtue Guardian says, "'I' and 'mine' form a dualism. Because there is an 'I,' there is also a 'mine.' But if there is no 'I,' then there will be no 'mine.' In this way one enters the gate of nondualism." The bodhisattva Lion, says, "Blame and blessing form a dualism. But if one penetrates the true nature of blame, it is no different from blessing. When one can dispose of forms with this diamondlike wisdom, neither bound nor liberated, one may in this way enter the gate of nondualism."[10]

Then Manjushri's turn comes. This is where the kong-an comes from. Manjushri says to all of them: "Good sirs, you have all spoken well. Nevertheless, all your explanations are themselves dualistic."[11]

He goes on:

"According to what I think, in all Dharmas no words, no speech, no revelation and no understanding, to let go all questions and answers: this is entering the not-two Dharma gate."

Then Manjusri asked Vimalakirti, "We have each already spoken. Now you should tell us, good man, what is a Bodhisattva's entry into the not two-dharma gate?"[12]

The sutra says, "At that time, Vimalakirti remained silent and did not speak a word." Manjushri sighed and said, "Excellent, excellent! Not a word, not a syllable—this truly is to enter the gate of non-dualism!"[13]

That is the teaching: Silence speaks louder than words.

But what does it say? Listen carefully. Listen!

Notes

1. See Seung Sahn, trans., *The Blue Cliff Record* (Cumberland, RI: Kwan Um School of Zen, 1983), 64.
2. Ibid.
3. Thomas Cleary and J. C. Cleary, trans., *The Blue Cliff Record* (Boston: Shambhala, 1992), 459.
4. Thomas Cleary, trans., *Book of Serenity* (Boston: Shambhala, 1988), 201.
5. In *Book of Serenity*, Cleary speaks of an awl rather than a digging tool.
6. Burton Watson, trans., *The Vimalakirti Sutra*, (New York: Columbia University Press, 1997), 37.
7. See Cheng Chien, trans., *Sun Face Buddha: The Teachings of Ma-tsu and the Hungchou School of Ch'an* (Berkeley, CA: Asian Humanities Press, 1992), 59–60.
8. Charles Luk, trans., *The Vimalakirti Nirdesa Sutra* (Boston: Shambhala, 1972), 90–91.
9. Ibid., 104.
10. Ibid., 104–05.
11. *The Holy Teaching of Vimalakirti*, trans. Robert A. F. Thurman (University Park: Pennsylvania State University Press, 1976), 77.
12. Seung Sahn, 64.
13. Watson, 111.

CHAPTER 21

The Diamond Sutra's Extinction
of Sinful Karma

The speech and words of all buddhas, bodhisatvas,
and great masters come from where?

The speech and words of all buddhas, bodhisatvas,
and great masters return to where?

Speech and words and the unnameable, are they
the same or different?

Haahh!!

In the evening a wooden chicken is crowing.

In the sky the bright moon is shining.

Case 97 in *The Blue Cliff Record* is titled, "The Diamond Sutra's Extinction of Sinful Karma." The case states that:

The Diamond Sutra says, "If one is scorned and disdained
by others, this person has made sinful karma in previous
lives, which should bring him down into the evil realms, but
because of the scorn and disdain by others in the present life,
the sinful karma of previous lives is thereby extinguished."[1]

This kong-an is a direct quote of a short section from the Diamond Sutra. And the Diamond Sutra itself is a short Buddhist scripture, perhaps twenty-five pages long in English, that was very much respected and used in China, Japan, and Korea. The Diamond Sutra is similar to the Heart Sutra, in that it is a teaching about emptiness.

In the kong-an, three things are referred to. The first is karma; the second is its allusion to the Diamond Sutra itself; the third is the transformative power of insult. Let's look at each of these briefly.

Karma is a favorite topic of new Zen students and people being introduced to Buddhism. (Another topic that stirs up a lot of curiosity and fascination is reincarnation.) The word *karma* comes from a Sanskrit root, which is connected with action—action and reaction, or cause and effect. The theory of cause-and-effect is based on a concept called dependent origination, which says that the origin of each thing is dependent on many other things. The simplest formulation of dependent origination says because of this, that, because of that, this. So any phenomenon that we encounter—whether it's ourself or another person, a thought, an idea, a chair, whatever it is—this thing is dependent on many other things that are not the thing itself. If you look into any situation, you can see that any particular phenomenon arises from many, many other things. For example, if you look at a flower from the perspective of the teachings contained in the Heart Sutra or the Diamond Sutra, you might infer that the flower is not a flower, because what makes up a flower are many nonflower elements: the sun, the earth, the water, the gardener who tended it, and so on. Thus the causes and conditions that generate the flower are multiple. A flower is not a flower, and therefore we can call it a flower. That is the style of the presentation in the Diamond Sutra. That is the teaching of dependent origination.

The idea of karma says that if we do something now, certain results will come later. So in looking at karma, there is always a past, a present, and a future.

In Buddhism you can find two ways of representing things. The first is that everything is changing, changing, changing, moment by moment by moment. It's something like watching a movie and seeing all kinds of movement going on. It appears that there is movement, but if you stop the film and look closely at what is generating the movement, you see just a series of individual, complete representations or images—one frame at a time, complete—one frame at a time, complete—on and on and on.

As the film moves, the appearance or illusion is of continuous motion. But if you stop the film and look closely, you see that there is just one complete frame, one complete frame, one complete frame. The moving aspect suggests dependent origination. You see that something from the past gives rise to something in the present gives rise to something in the future. If you plant corn seed, corn will come up later.

The second way of representing things is that each thing is just as it is and is not dependent on something else that has changed into what is now. It's just as it is, like each complete frame in the film strip. That is the notion of nature origination: Moment by moment, each thing is complete and is an expression of original nature.

If you can look at something, whether it's yourself or some phenomenon outside yourself, and view it from both perspectives, then you see the whole truth. But if you get caught up in seeing only the form and movement, then you miss the suchness of each moment.

So what we do now gives rise to certain conditions and causes later. And of course, if you take a very wide view, then every primary cause is not necessarily going to bear fruit in a short period of time. So the notion of reincarnation emerges, that some causes will take many lifetimes to come to fruition. There is a certain ethical value to that way of looking at things. If you see that what you do now is the cause of what you reap later, then you have to take responsibility for where you are just now, because the implication is that what I did in the past has led me to this situation now. Further, the situation that I find myself in now is a teaching of some kind that will lead to greater development and unfoldment. This fosters a view of self-responsibility rather than self-pity.

The saying "It's just my karma" has become common parlance in English. But just because karma implies self-responsibility, that doesn't mean you look at someone who is suffering and fold your arms and say, Well, that's their karma; I've got nothing to do with it. Your karma at that moment consists of causes and conditions that have brought you to interface with this being who is suffering or in need. How then will you respond? Karma does not imply a rigid attitude of "I'll take care of myself and you take care of yourself." Quite the contrary.

The section of the Diamond Sutra that is used as a kong-an here is referred to as "transforming wrongdoing and becoming enlightened." It was traditionally considered capable of clearing away karmic obstructions. So if someone really looked into this short paragraph, it could remove hindrances.

An early teacher in China, Great Teacher Fu (Daishi; Bu Dae Sa), had a verse on this section:

> In a previous embodiment there were consequential
>   hindrances;
> Today accepting and upholding this scripture,
> Temporarily slighted and scorned by people,
> It turns the serious back into light.[2]

A story about Zen Master Chao-chou (Joshu; Joju) illustrates the transformative value of insult. Chao-chou and Bunon decided one day to have a contest to see who was best at demeaning themselves. The winner would be the loser—that is, the one who could demean himself the most. Further, the winner was then to buy a rice cake for the loser.

> Joshu said, "I'm a donkey."
> Bunon said, "I am the donkey's ass."
> Joshu said, "I am the donkey's dung."
> Bunon said, "I am the worm in the dung."
> Joshu said, "What's the good of being there?"
> Bunon said, "I spend the summer there."
> Joshu said, "Go buy a ricecake!" [Bunon had won the contest.][3]

Traditionally monks and nuns in China and Korea spend two ninety-day periods each year sitting retreat. One is in the winter, and the other is from late spring into early summer. Spending the summer there means sitting the summer retreat there, as a worm in the donkey's crap. That was enough for Chao-chou, and he declared his friend the winner.

Sitting retreat as a worm in the donkey's dung is the condition of our life and our practice. Our practice is not to find some exalted state somewhere else, free of any kind of impurity and pain. Our practice is to pursue something and find our true way right in the middle of all the crap of this life. According to this section of the sutra, which talks repeatedly about sinful karma, if you are scorned and disdained by others, if you receive all kinds of insults from others, you have made sinful karma in previous lives, which should bring you down into the evil realms. (Entering evil realms means being reborn as a demon or ghost or animal—something less than human.) But because of the scorn and the disdain by others in this life, the sinful karma of previous lives is extinguished. You are free. So if you want to help those closest to you, you should tell your wife or husband, your boyfriend or girlfriend, your sister or brother, what absolute assholes they are! Then you will free them of their sinful karma of previous lives and help them with their practice. That is the point. Accepting the pain of scorn or insult more or less evens the scales.

One more aspect of rebirth should be clarified: Everything is not totally determined. Your current life is based on your previous actions, but your current choices of response are not. What you do now generates where you will be later—what kind of situation you will encounter, whom you will come into contact with—but how you respond in that situation is still up to you.

Sometimes the working of karma is described in terms of primary cause and secondary conditions. If you practice meditation and come to a point where your mind is not moving, not generating notions of past, present, and future, and if you return to that point over and over again, then much of the energy that was being pumped into some particular primary cause, like anger or greed, is redirected. That cause gradually loses its generating power, with the result that you aren't so influenced by it anymore.

But that doesn't necessarily mean you can get rid of every condition. If you were born, for example, with one arm, and there is some primary cause in your past life that generated your being born in this life with only one arm, you can sit in meditation till the cows come home, but you are never going to gain that other arm. You are not going to change your karma in that way. But what can change is how you respond to that situation. How you respond can be based on staying in the present moment.

The basic teaching of the sutra is that all things are originally empty and all signs or characteristics that we see temporarily are essentially delusion. That means that karma is also originally empty. An illusory cause produces an illusory result. If you watch a film strip and believe the action to be total reality, that is called missing the real and clinging to the illusory. You are missing the fact that essentially there is no action, only a series of frames, one following the next. The sutra's advice is not to get caught by signs, not to cling to concepts.

Once there was a lion cub whose mother was killed. The cub ran away and found itself amidst a flock of sheep. The sheep took in the lion cub, and some of the mother sheep nursed it. The lion cub grew up with these sheep and did everything that sheep do. When predators came, it ran just like the sheep. When the sheep bleated, it learned to bleat. It was living its life as a sheep. One day a lion appeared, and all the sheep started to run. This lion saw the other lion running with the sheep and thought it strange. He caught up with the lion who thought it was a sheep and said, "What are you doing? You're a lion. Why are you running with the sheep?" And the lion said, "No, no, no. I'm a sheep!" The lion took the sheep-lion to a pond and made it look into the water. Seeing its reflection, it saw that it was indeed a lion.

We all attach to labels about ourselves: I'm good; I'm not so good; I'm better than everyone else; I'm worse than everyone else. The list goes on and on and on, but those are all images, and fundamentally they are delusion. We get caught in them and don't see the essential self that is there before signs and designations.

The sutra is called the Diamond Sutra—the diamond that cuts through delusion. Diamonds are hard and can cut through anything, and they can also reflect all phenomena. The diamond that cuts through delusion is essentially the mind-sword of don't-know that we keep directing ourselves back to in our meditation practice.

Once in ancient China, the emperor invited Great Teacher Fu to the palace to lecture on the Diamond Sutra. The whole court assembled in the dharma hall. Great Teacher Fu came in, walked to the front, mounted the rostrum, took hold of the lectern, shook it hard once— *pkuh!*—and then got down and walked out.

The emperor stood there dumbfounded. His first minister—Minister Chih—said, "Does your majesty understand?"

The emperor said, "No, I don't understand."

Minister Chih said, "Great Teacher Fu has completed his exposition on the Diamond Sutra."

The essential point of the Diamond Sutra was revealed through Great Teacher Fu's action. The sutra iterates over and over several core ideas. One is that true practice is not holding on to any idea or image of a self, a person, a living being, or a life span, because all those create the feeling of separation from the situation we are actually in. If you hold the notion of a self, then you have I and not-I. If you hold the notion of a person, then you think, I'm a person, and there are nonperson things here. But where actually does self end and not-self begin? Where does person end and not-person begin? Where do living beings end and nonliving things begin? We all know that ecologically speaking we are dependent on many things that are considered not living beings. And likewise if you hold to the notion of a life span, then you think there is life, which is one thing, and death, which is another thing. But in the great round mind mirror, all things are equally reflected. The sutra emphasizes this point. Don't make an image of self, person, living being, or life span.

The Diamond Sutra also emphasizes that all appearances and signs are illusory and deceptive. If you see that all appearances are not true characteristics, then you will see true nature. Or you could say that if you see the signless quality of signs, then you see your true self.

Essentially that means that the actual quality of just seeing is your true self—not some image but the just-seeing, the perception itself; perceiving is who and what you are. If you try to objectify yourself and find yourself in some image, you are continuously chasing something that is delusion.

The sutra also emphasizes giving rise to an intention with a mind that does not dwell anywhere. In Zen practice, we frequently emphasize making a firm intention to practice, to help others, to cut through delusions, and to use all things as teachings. But if you take any of these intentions as being substantive, then you have already missed the true spirit of intention. The sutra cautions against that. To emphasize this point, it posits that there is no independently existing object of mind called highest awakening or bodhisattva. Further, it says that what is called the Buddha's teaching is not the Buddha's teaching.

When Zen Master Te-shan (Tokusan; Dok Sahn) was a young monk, he was a scholar of the Diamond Sutra. He heard that in the south of China some monks were practicing Zen, practicing meditation, sitting facing the wall as if they were asleep and claiming that they got enlightenment. He thought this was heretical and decided he would pack up his commentaries on the Diamond Sutra and go to the south and teach these monks the true way. So he put his packs on his back and set out on foot. One day he stopped at a small roadside tea house. The proprietress was an old woman. She saw his packs and could see there were scrolls in them, so she asked him, "What do you have in there?"

He said, "Those are my commentaries on the Diamond Sutra."

She said, "Oh, you understand the Diamond Sutra?"

He said yes.

She said, "If you can answer one question about the Diamond Sutra, then you can have your lunch for free. But if you can't answer my question, then I won't serve you, and you will have to leave."

Te-shan pulled himself up and rather arrogantly said, "Any question."

The old woman said, "In the sutra it says, 'Past mind cannot get enlightenment, present mind cannot get enlightenment, future mind cannot get enlightenment.' So I ask you, with what kind of mind will you eat lunch?"

Te-shan was stuck and didn't know what to say. When he got over his embarrassment, he asked her, "Is there a Zen master in this vicinity?"

And she said, "Yes. Down the road five miles is the temple of the well-known teacher Lung-t'an (Ryutan; Yong Dam)." Te-shan went there and became Lung-t'an's student.

The sutra says, "All compound things are like a dream, a phantom, a drop of dew, a flash of lightning. Thus should we observe them." It also says that "the tathagata, or the realized one, does not come from anywhere and does not go to anywhere." The usual translation of the Sanskrit word *tathagata* is "thus come one" or "thus gone one," but here it translates it as the one that does not come from anywhere and does not go to anywhere. That means that when you completely see the actuality of this moment, then you realize that there is essentially no coming and no going. And in that recognition you realize the true suchness of yourself and all things.

Zen calls that "moment mind." Moment mind is what is most emphasized in the Zen tradition. Sometimes it is referred to as one mind or original mind.

Zen Master Yuan-wu (Engo) said, "Myriad things all come forth from one's own mind. One moment of thought is aware; once aware, it pervades; having pervaded, it transforms. An Ancient said, 'The green bamboos are all true thusness; the lush yellow flowers are all wisdom.'"[4]

The Sixth Patriarch has the most radical view of the section of the sutra used as a kong-an. The sutra says, "If one is scorned and disdained by others, this person has made sinful karma in previous lives." The Sixth Patriarch said, "'Previous ages' is the deluded mind of the preceding moment; 'the present age' is the awake mind of the succeeding moment. The awake mind of the succeeding moment scorns the deluded mind of the previous moment; because the delusion cannot remain, therefore it is said that the wicked deeds of previous ages will thereby be dissolved."[5]

The sutra says *scorns*, but you could see the delusion of the last moment and just burst out laughing. Because you perceive the delusion of the previous moment, that delusion cannot remain, so the sinful karma of previous lives is dissolved. The Sixth Patriarch is not much interested in some grand notion of reincarnation. Previous life is the preceding moment in which you are holding some deluded image of yourself or some idea or concept.

This moment is the awake mind, just now. In this awake moment, you see clearly right through—*ptchh*—like a diamond cutting through delusion. So if you come to this moment mind, then you see your true nature.

There is one last point to be made. The sutra refers over and over to karma. But the essence of the sutra is that all forms are empty. So that means that karma is also empty.

If karma is also dependent on many other things and is empty of its own self-nature, then just now, where does karma come from?

Open your mouth, already a mistake.

Notes

1. Seung Sahn, trans., *The Blue Cliff Record* (Cumberland, RI: Kwan Um School of Zen, 1983), 74.
2. Thomas Cleary, trans., *Book of Serenity* (Boston: Shambhala, 1988), 244.
3. Yoel Hoffmann, trans., *Radical Zen: The Sayings of Joshu* (Brookline, MA: Autumn Press, 1978), 145.
4. Thomas Cleary and J. C. Cleary, trans., *The Blue Cliff Record* (Boston: Shambhala, 1992), 535.
5. Cleary, 245.

CHAPTER 22

Aspects of Failure: A Woman Comes Out of Samadhi

Mistake.

Failure.

These designations come from where?

Haahh!!

Why do you make all that? What are you doing just now?

In the *Wu-men-kuan* (*Mumonkan; Mu Mun Kwan*), case 42 is based on a fable derived from a Buddhist scripture. Zen Master Wu-men takes this story and uses it as a kong-an:

Once, long ago, Mun Su Bosal went to a gathering of all Buddhas. Just then, all the Buddhas returned to their original seats. Only one woman remained, seated near Shakyamuni Buddha, deep in samadhi.

Mun Su Sari [Bosal] asked the Buddha, "Why can a woman sit so close to you, and I cannot?" The Buddha told Mun Su Sari, "You wake her up from samadhi and ask her yourself."

Mun Su Sari walked around the woman three times and snapped his fingers. Then, he took her in the palm of his hand, carried her to Heaven, and used transcendent energy on her, but could not wake her up.

Buddha said, "If one hundred Mun Su Saris appeared, they also could not wake her up. Down below, past twelve hundred million countries, there is Ma Myung Bosal, who will be able to wake her up from samadhi."

Immediately, Ma Myung Bosal emerged out of the earth and bowed to the Buddha, who gave him the command. Ma Myung walked in front of the woman and snapped his fingers only once. At this, the woman woke up from samadhi and stood up from her seat.[1]

That is the case. Then there is a short poem:

> Come out, not come out,
> Both are already free.
> God's head and demon's face.
> The failure, how elegant.[2]

This story has a cast of characters. One is Shakyamuni Buddha, the historical Buddha. Another is Mun Su Sari Bosal, also known as Manjushri Bodhisattva. He represents the enlightened nature of universal, primordial wisdom. Another character is Ma Myung Bosal. *Bosal* means "bodhisattva," so he too is an enlightened being. *Ma Myung* translates as "ensnared light." Ensnared Light Bodhisattva is nowhere near as lofty and celestial as Manjushri; he emerges from earth. Finally, there is a woman sitting in deep meditative absorption. In India at that time, women were generally regarded as second-class citizens. That is why the question appears, "Why can a woman sit so close to you, and I cannot?"

A long time ago, according to the story, in some distant land not of our realm, all the buddhas had a convocation. But, although Manjushri was traditionally called the teacher of the seven buddhas, he had not been invited to this gathering. Because Manjushri represents wisdom, it follows that the teacher of all buddhas is clear wisdom. Of course, all of this is allegorical, so actually we are being represented here.

We are told that Manjushri was not invited to this convocation of the Buddhas but finally was allowed to enter. Just as he did so, all the other buddhas returned to their original places, wherever the original place of all buddhas might be. (Maybe we will find that place sometime in our Zen meditation.) As they return, only a woman remains. Seated near Shakyamuni, she is in deep *samadhi*, deep meditation. She does not know anything; she does not hear anything; she is just at one with everything. Manjushri asks the Buddha, "Why can this woman sit so close to you, and I cannot?" The Buddha replies, "Why don't you wake her up from samadhi and ask her yourself?" Manjushri tries to do so, using all of his powers, but the woman does not move at all.

Now, the reason she does not move is because Manjushri represents the realm of total, absolute equality. In total equality, there is no going into and no coming out of; there is no before and no after. Of course he can't wake her, because he is immersed in total equality. Then the Buddha says, in effect, "Even if a hundred of you, even if a thousand of you appeared, still you wouldn't be able to wake her up," because Manjushri represents the zero point. Even if you have a hundred zeroes or a thousand zeroes, they still equal zero.

"But down below," Buddha continues, "past hundreds of millions of countries [meaning not in this celestial realm, but on earth] there is another bodhisattva. His name is Ensnared Light [another translation of his name is Deluded Consciousness]. He can awaken her." You see, this bodhisattva understands about coming and going, entering into and leaving from, all the things that are not of Manjushri's realm. Just then, Ensnared Light Bodhisattva emerges from earth. This is a wonderful image: Out of earth emerges a bodhisattva. (Our practice, of course, always has to be rooted in this solid earth.) When the bodhisattva emerges, Buddha gives him the command. He walks up, snaps his fingers once, and the woman awakens.

After the case and poem is Wu-men's prose comment:

Buddha acted out a complex play, having nothing in common with minor trivia.

Now tell me: Manjushri was the teacher of seven Buddhas; why couldn't he get the woman out of absorption? Ensnared Light was a bodhisattva of the first stage; why was he able to get her out?

If you can see intimately here [that is, in first-hand experience], you will attain the great dragonic absorption even in the flurry of active consciousness.[3]

The last line is particularly interesting. If you can see intimately here, into this point—why one could get her out and the other could not—then you will attain great samadhi, great absorption, like a powerful dragon, even in the flurry of active consciousness.

Other translations give different versions of that last line. If you combine them, the nuance of the comment emerges more strongly. A second translation says, "If you can see into this intimately, then in the flurry of karma and discrimination you are a dragon of great samadhi."[4] Then, a third one: "If you can grasp this completely, you will realize that surging delusive consciousness is nothing other than the greatest samadhi."[5] And the last one: "If you can firmly grasp this point, then for you this busy life of ignorance and discrimination will be the life of supreme satori."[6] I like this last one best, because it relates to "this busy life of ignorance and discrimination," which we all know only too well.

The poem's different versions also show interesting nuances. Our version says:

Come out, not come out,
Both are already free.
God's head and demon's face.
The failure, how elegant.[7]

Another version of this same poem reads:

One can awaken her, the other cannot;
Both have their own freedom.
A god-mask here and a devil-mask there;
Even in failure, an elegant performance.[8]

Commenting on the second line, Yamada Roshi, the translator, writes, "Take the example of a jet plane about to take off. A hundred thousand Manjushris might not be able to get it started, but a jet pilot could do so very easily."[9]

This kong-an focuses us on the various forms of failure. When we read Zen stories, the usual focus is one of success; someone usually gets enlightened. But there is often another aspect. Once, a long time ago, Shakyamuni Buddha was about to give his dharma speech on Vulture Peak, where twelve hundred people were assembled, including monks, nuns, laywomen, and laymen. They waited and waited for Buddha to give his talk, but Buddha did not say anything. He just sat silently on the rostrum. The audience was expectant. Finally the Buddha picked up a flower and held it up. We are told that no one understood except Mahakashyapa, who smiled. Then Buddha said, "I have the all-pervading true dharma, exquisite teaching of formless form and incomparable nirvana, a special transmission outside the sutras, not dependent on words and speech. This I give to you, Mahakashyapa."

That is a story of success for Mahakashyapa, who understood the Buddha's gesture. But what about the other 1,199 people? They also attained something, sitting there wondering, What is the Buddha's speech? When he held up a flower, no one understood, so they all attained don't-understand, don't-know. That was their success. Mahakashyapa got the transmission and a very hard job! The rest of them got don't-know mind. Who succeeded and who failed?

On a recent visit to China, I went to the temple of the Sixth Patriarch in the south. On my return I reread the Platform Sutra of the Sixth Patriarch, which contains the teachings he gave in the town where the temple is located. The Platform Sutra tells the story of a poetry contest. The Fifth Patriarch, realizing that he was aging, decided to give his robe and bowl, along with succession of the dharma, to the monk who could write a poem demonstrating true understanding of the essence of mind. When the head monk heard that challenge, he thought to himself, "I know that the other monks are not going to write poems because they assume that I am the best qualified. I wonder whether I should try to write a poem or not. If I don't write a poem showing my mind to the patriarch, then how will he know whether my understanding is superficial or deep? If I write a poem with the intention of just getting the dharma succession, then my motive would be pure. But if, on the other hand, I write the poem trying to get the patriarchy, then I'll be no different from a common, materialistic person who's just interested in name and fame. That wouldn't be good. If, however, I don't try, how will I get the dharma?" He thought about this repeatedly and worked himself into an agitated state.

This dialogue he has with himself is interesting. He questions motive and weighs sincerity of effort. He is penetrating and honest in asking himself these questions. For most of us, of course, motivation is rarely a pure thing. But from a Zen perspective, there is a difference between purity and clarity. If one has purity, then everything is simple—like white paper. But most of us have mixed, complex motives when we set out to do something. If, at the root of our various complex motives, there is a sense of clear direction about the essential reason we are pursuing something, then our direction and motive are clear, even if not simple. That is an important point in Zen practice: Our sense of direction should always be clear. Even if the motive is not always completely pure and simple, the direction should be determined by the question, Why do I do this?

In our story, the head monk finally wrote a poem and went to the patriarch's room to present it. But when he reached the door, he became agitated and broke out in a sweat. He could not knock on the door. He went to the door thirteen times in the course of four days and could not bring himself to go in. Finally the monk thought to himself, "I'll go to the corridor in front of the patriarch's room in the middle of the night, and there I'll write my poem on the wall. If the patriarch sees it and approves it, I'll come out, pay homage to him, and let him know I wrote the poem. If, on the other hand, he doesn't approve it, then I've wasted years practicing at this temple. What a sorry condition." At midnight, carrying a candle, he arrived in front of the patriarch's room and wrote this poem:

Body is the Bodhi Tree,
Mind is clear mirror's stand,
Always clean, clean, clean,
Don't keep dust.[10]
[The Buddha sat under the bodhi tree when he got his
    enlightenment experience.]

After writing the poem on the wall, he returned quickly to his room so no one would see him. He sat, again in a state of agitation, thinking, "I wonder whether the patriarch will find any merit in my poem. If he does, I'm ready to receive the dharma from him. If he doesn't, that means that I'm not a good vessel to receive the dharma because my mind is still clouded and befuddled with bad karma from previous lifetimes." He sat the whole night like that, without sleeping, wondering what was going to happen.

Now, the patriarch's room faced an area with three corridors. The patriarch had commissioned an artist from the imperial court to paint the corridors with portraits of the different patriarchs and images representing stories from the Buddhist sutras. In the morning the patriarch came out of his room with the artist and saw the verse on the wall. The patriarch told the artist, "Better to not paint these hallways at all. I'm sorry that I brought you all this way, but the Diamond Sutra says all forms are empty, so why put anything on the walls. We should just all look at this verse and pay homage to it."

The patriarch instructed all the monks to learn this verse, saying that practicing it would help them get enlightenment in the future. But he did not say, This verse demonstrates the essence of mind. The verse, you may notice, talks about purification: The body is the Bodhi tree, the mind is the clear mirror's stand; constantly we should clean them, so that no dust collects. That's not bad; it's better than making a mess. But it has the notion of time in it, before and after, impurity moving toward purity—a kind of self-improvement campaign.

At midnight the Fifth Patriarch sent for the head monk and asked, "Did you write the poem?"—knowing full well that he had. He also knew that the monk had not really attained enlightenment. The monk said, "Yes, I wrote the poem. I don't dare seek your patriarchy, but please tell me whether this poem has any merit to it or not." The patriarch told him, "You have gotten to the door of enlightenment, but you have not gone through." And he added, "The essence of mind is to be spontaneously realized as something which is before coming and going, cleaning or not cleaning. My suggestion is that you return to your room and ponder this more deeply for a few days. If you see into the true nature of your being, then write me another poem, and I will transmit the dharma and the patriarchy to you." The head monk went back to his room and tried very, very hard to write another poem, based on his intuition. But he just got more and more perturbed and could not produce anything.

Then, we are told, the Sixth Patriarch-to-be wrote his poem on the wall:

> Bodhi has no tree.
> Clear mirror has no stand.
> Originally nothing.
> Where is dust?[11]

He succeeded where the head monk failed. But we should recognize the monk's effort and be inspired by his honesty and humility. These qualities are very, very important in pursuing practice.

Failure is actually a most important aspect of Zen practice, because when you truly fail, at that moment you stop relating to practice as something that is going to get you somewhere. And even in the midst of your failure, if you continue to practice rather than giving up and throwing the whole thing out the window, then practice becomes your way of life. In fact, practice becomes your life. Practice just becomes practice. Out of that, the spirit of compassionate activity also is born, because if you truly embrace what failure is, the heart of kindness begins to emerge. If you cannot face your own failure, then it is difficult to face the failings of anyone else.

Eido Roshi tells a story about a monk he once observed in a temple in Japan. Roshi watched this monk sweeping the courtyard every day and going about his simple activities. Roshi was taken by the non-specialness of it all; the monk's decorum was impressive in its ordinariness. Finally he approached the monk, thinking that he must be really advanced in kong-an practice, and asked, "What kong-an do you work on?" The monk replied, "Well, to tell you the truth, all these years I've never passed the first kong-an, Mu."

We find another inspiring failure in the Christian story of Easter. When Jesus is in the Garden of Gethsemane with all his disciples, he tells them that one of them will betray him that very night and soldiers will come and arrest him. Peter, his foremost disciple, speaks up and says, "Lord, why cannot I follow thee now? I will lay down my life for thy sake." Jesus answers him, "Verily, verily, I say unto thee, the cock shall not crow, till thou hast denied me thrice."[12] Then the soldiers come and arrest Jesus and take him to the prison. Peter follows along behind to see what is happening. While he is standing outside the prison, he is asked three times, "Aren't you one of the followers of Jesus of Nazareth?" "I know not the man," he declares. "And immediately the cock crew."[13]

What follows after the arrest and crucifixion of Jesus is very interesting: Peter goes on to become the successor. He becomes the first pope. Imagine what that must have felt like, to have completely denied knowing your teacher and then to have the fortitude to carry on his tradition. It is a wonderful example of not being daunted by failure and weakness.

One more poem commenting on this case comes from a later Zen master, Langya:

The woman, Manjushri, and Ensnared Light:
Ultimately how do Zen followers understand?

Only if you harmonize subtly, beyond convention,

Will you believe the waves are basically water.[14]

I hope that we all fail miserably and perceive clearly that the waves were never separate from the water.

Notes

1. Seung Sahn, trans., *The Mu Mun Kwan* (Cumberland, RI: Kwan Um School of Zen, 1983), 49.
2. Ibid., 50.
3. Thomas Cleary, trans., *No Barrier* (New York: Bantam, 1993), 186.
4. Robert Aitken, trans., *The Gateless Barrier* (San Francisco: North Point Press, 1991), 257.
5. Koun Yamada, trans., *The Gateless Gate* (Boston: Wisdom, 2004), 200.
6. Zenkei Shibayama, *The Gateless Barrier* (Boston: Shambhala, 2000), 294.
7. Seung Sahn, 50.
8. Yamada, 203.
9. Ibid.
10. Seung Sahn, *The Whole World Is a Single Flower* (Rutland, VT: Tuttle, 1992), 220.
11. Ibid.
12. John 13:38.
13. Matt. 26:74.
14. Cleary, 186.

About the Author

Richard Shrobe (Zen Master Wu Kwang) is the guiding teacher of the Chogye International Zen Center of New York. He has been teaching in the Kwan Um School of Zen, the largest Zen organization in North America, for over twenty-five years. He is one of the first American students to receive transmission from Zen Master Seung Sahn, who was the Seventy-Eighth Patriarch in his line of dharma transmission in the Chogye order of Korean Buddhism.

Before practicing Zen, Shrobe studied intensively with Swami Satchidananda, living with his wife and children for four years at the Integral Yoga Institute in New York. He became a student of Zen Master Seung Sahn in 1975 and received *inka*, or formal certification to teach Zen, in 1984. Shrobe is a certified Gestalt psychotherapist and instructor with a master's degree in social work. He was formerly a professional jazz musician who did his undergraduate training in music theory and studied jazz piano with Barry Harris.

Shrobe lives in New York with his family and has a private practice in psychotherapy. He is the author of *Open Mouth Already a Mistake* and *Don't-Know Mind: The Spirit of Korean Zen*.

Index

Printed in the United States
by Baker & Taylor Publisher Services